Praise for *All Feelings Welcome*

"As a child psychiatrist and advocate for children's mental health, I am deeply impressed by Kelly and Callie's book on parenting. This book is a treasure trove of wisdom, blending therapeutic principles with practical strategies that empower parents to support their children's emotional development from the earliest stages. I appreciate how this book, written by authors with a deep understanding of child development, addresses common parenting challenges and provides a roadmap for fostering a child's self-esteem, resilience, and empathy. This expertise shines through in every chapter, making this a must-read for anyone looking to nurture their child's emotional well-being. Kelly and Callie have created a unique and valuable resource that will positively impact families everywhere. I highly recommend this book to parents, caregivers, and educators seeking to create a nurturing and emotionally supportive environment for children."

—**Helen Egger**, MD., Co-founder and Chief Medical & Scientific Officer at Little Otter, www.littleotterhealth.com

"*All Feelings Welcome* is the parenting book that we need today! It provides you with the tools that you need to feel empowered and to take an active role in helping guide your children gain the confidence they need to navigate life and all the emotions that come along with it. I can't wait to share this book with my mom friends and colleagues and also recommend it to clients."

—**Rachel L. Goldman**, PhD, FTOS, FASMBS-IH, licensed psychologist, speaker, and Clinical Assistant Professor in the Department of Psychiatry at NYU Grossman School of Medicine

"All I've ever wanted as a parent is to be the best support system to my child so that they can fully grow into the person they were meant to be. With *All Feelings Welcome*, Kelly and Callie have given us a treasure trove of ways to help our kids embrace and develop their emotional well-being, and maybe even do a bit of healing ourselves along the way! This is an incredibly empowering read for anyone on their parenting journey."

—**Jason Ritter**, actor and voice of Fox's Dad on the Emmy-nominated Apple TV+ series *Slumberkins*

"*All Feelings Welcome* is a must-have book for all parents and caregivers! Kelly and Callie have crafted the ultimate practical, empowering tool to help you build and support healthy emotional well-being with your children and caregivers. You can't go wrong with this wonderful offering from the creators behind the lovable Slumberkins brand."

—**Yvette Nicole Brown**, actress and Slumberkins superfan

"This book is what I wanted for all the parents whose kids went to school with my kids. This book makes me hopeful for parents and caregivers and humans so when their kids experience any kind of emotions, they can guide them (and themselves) through the feelings, navigating and embracing all the scary, underwhelming, and overwhelming things life throws at them. I wish this book was published 20 years ago. Or 50 years ago. . . ."

—**Pamela Adlon**, voice of Fox's Mom on the Emmy-nominated
Apple TV+ series *Slumberkins*

"*All Feelings Welcome* is a must-have book for parents and caregivers looking to support emotional resilience in their kids. Practical, inspiring, and easy to implement, the strategies in this book will help you and your kids build positive connections wherever life takes you. *All Feelings Welcome* is truly a book everyone needs to read!"

—**Allie Szczecinski**, MSEd,
Founder of Miss Behavior

"This is an indispensable goldmine for parents! *All Feelings Welcome* leads us down the path to emotional resilience, demonstrating the ways we can best help our kids face whatever life throws their way in a confident, capable manner. The creators of Slumberkins have outdone themselves with the clear, actionable strategies in this book. Every parent needs this book!"

—**Jon Gustin**, The Tired Dad

All Feelings Welcome

All Feelings Welcome

PARENTING PRACTICES FOR RAISING CARING, CONFIDENT, AND RESILIENT KIDS

Kelly Oriard
Callie Christensen

We dedicate this book to each and every member in our SlumberFam community who has come to us for support and found the community, inspiration, and confidence to change the way we support the emotional wellness of the next generation—because it takes a village. You are the beating heart of Slumberkins.

And to the SlumberKids out there . . . we can't wait to watch as you continue becoming the caring, confident, resilient human beings you already are.

CONTENTS

Hello to all of you parents, caregivers, and educators! We are thrilled to welcome you into our first-ever Slumberkins parenting book. Whether you are already a part of the SlumberFam or you've never heard of Slumberkins before reading this, we're so happy you're here.

When we set out to build Slumberkins, we wanted to boil down complicated therapeutic, educational, and philosophical theories into bite-sized chunks that are as easy to use as reading a book, hugging a plush, or watching a show. We created these done-for-you shortcuts so that you can focus on what really matters: being the best parent you can be.

The Slumberkins Connect-to-Grow approach can be taught from the moment a child is born. It's designed to be both comforting for children and a resource for adults to take the lead in a child's social-emotional development. We designed it in this way because a child's emotional wellness is interconnected with important adults in their lives, and we wanted to support children *and* families in their emotional wellness.

Even though you might be familiar with the Slumberkins books, toys, plush, music–and even an Emmy-nominated show on AppleTV+--you may not be aware that below the surface is a rich therapeutic and educational foundation. And that's exactly how we planned it to be.

But if you know the Slumberkins world, you may *want* to know why we suggest using affirmations. You may want to know how we arrived at our methods. Being informed of the theory and the *why* behind our approach may help you feel more knowledgeable when using it with your children.

We were inspired to write this book to demonstrate all of the therapeutic benefits that were built into the foundation of the brand, each character, and piece of content that we put out there. All of that comes back to the ideas in this book. Each character in our Slumberkins universe is a part of a bigger picture, a concrete way to approach the emotional development of our children.

Previously these theories and methods were mostly available in family therapy sessions. We want to embed the same concepts that experts use into tools that are available to everyone to use at home.

Don't panic if you aren't familiar with Slumberkins–we will be sharing tips and strategies you can use and practice in your daily life as a parent or caregiver even without our books and plush characters.

We will show you a roadmap for proactively forming a positive foundation for your child's emotional health as well as effective strategies for navigating any bumps along the way.

W e are a former family therapist and special education teacher . . . and we had planned to retire that way. Never did we imagine that we would partner to form the educational brand and content company of our dreams.

Our story starts way back to high school when two awkward tall girls on the first day of volleyball tryouts just happened to become best friends. Since that day, our lives have generally run in a parallel direction: we both played Division 1 college sports on athletic scholarships, we both started our Master's programs in the world of education, and we both have kids around the same ages.

Kelly became a marriage and family therapist and school counselor. She spent her career working as a school counselor at a Title 1 School, mainly focusing on pre-k to middle school age children. In that environment, she focused on connecting the school with families, while supporting the mental and emotional health of everyone involved.

Callie became a special education and elementary school teacher, spending most of her career working in the world of special education at a K to 12 therapeutic day treatment school. (It's a very small setting that some school districts have that focuses on the mental and emotional health of students who are struggling with being safe and successful in a typical school environment.)

Then, serendipitously, we landed on maternity leave at the same time. Kelly had just had her first baby and Callie had just had her second. We would meet up and go on daily walks with the new babies, and oftentimes we would share stories and strategies that we were seeing in the schools.

There was one walk in particular when we had an "ah-ha" lightbulb moment. While our babies slept in their strollers, we realized that there were two simple things that made students in our programs more successful:

1. That the parents or primary caregiver were not only involved in the support, but that they also took an active role in the process of supporting the mental and emotional needs of the child. *But* most parents didn't know how to do this, they were afraid of messing up, and they were too overwhelmed to take initiative and research how to do it for themselves.

2. A student's perception of Self and their inner voice and world—their self-concept—was the key component of their ability to be successful. We knew developmentally that the inner voice is formed between the ages of 0 and 7, which means that these are the years you can make the biggest impact.

As we talked, we realized that there weren't many turn-key resources available to help families address these two things. Most of what we saw was curriculum-based—designed for educators, not parents.

At the same time, we knew that almost every family we worked with in the schools looked to us as the experts to "fix," or support, their child. Unknowingly, they were giving their power away, simply because they didn't know how to meet the emotional needs underlying the behaviors or situations we saw their child exhibit in a school setting. Kelly, in her capacity as a family therapist, knew that anything we did, while beneficial, could be even more impactful. The key was empowering a parent or family member to say and do the therapeutic intervention with the child. The parent would have a much bigger impact than the counselor because of the connection they already have with the child. This is why we often say, "Parents are the best teachers of their child's emotional health and wellness."

While discussing this, and looking at our infant sons snuggling some of their favorite loveys, we had the idea to try and imbue some of the therapeutic tools and strategies into storylines with unique plush creatures and see what we could come up with that would empower parents to take the lead.

To start, we infused a progressive muscle relaxation routine into a storyline with a sweet Sloth to help parents support their children in creating a mind-body connection at bedtime.

We also made a Bigfoot (we *are* from the Pacific Northwest, after all!) who needed some help with self-esteem. We created an interactive narrative therapy story that brought affirmations to life and supported coping with hurt feelings. . .of Bigfoot, and inevitably the child being read to.

Once we had the stories, we taught ourselves how to sew and started selling the books and stories at local craft fairs—mainly to other moms and educators. The "how" Slumberkins came to be is a whole different story for another time, but what we found in these early days was that the stories *worked*.

We would get message after message online from parents asking for more—more stories, more characters, and more resources—that after a couple years, it was time for us to pursue Slumberkins full-time. We built a brand that didn't exist in the world yet—one that approached children's mental and emotional health in a way that had never been done before. We took a step back, zoomed out, and asked ourselves as a therapist, educator, and mothers, what library of resources and content we would want to proactively build a child's emotional wellness, while supporting the parents in taking the lead in teaching these important skills.

What exists today is that foundation, roadmap, and approach for how to easily implement this into your everyday parenting life.

ACKNOWLEDGMENTS

Thank you to our children who have inspired this whole dream and multiple Slumberkins stories and creatures—Aidan, Oliver, Logan, Henry, Owen, and Cora. You push us and inspire us every day to walk the walk and be better mothers and people in the world. This whole journey would not be possible had we not had the serendipitous maternity leaves with Aidan and Owen—you two boys were the catalysts who gave us the gift of time together and inspiration to turn this idea into a reality.

To our parents—we are forever grateful to each of you for giving us the opportunities that have led us toward our own paths of emotional growth and healing.

As Slumberkins has grown and evolved, we have brought in additional educational and therapeutic experts and thought leaders to help build the roadmap. Thank you to our therapeutic leadership teammates and contributors Sarah Block, Kimberly Allen, Krista Olson, Claire LaPoma, and Cicely Rodgers, who have been our partners and peers (even before Slumberkins); they've been working behind the scenes in building the content and curriculum that exists today. Your contributions have helped create the continually expanding tools and resources that have an incredible impact on the lives of parents, educators, and children.

Alissa Kramer, thank you for contributing your deeply personal and vulnerable story and experience to this book and being on this journey with us. Vanesa Holfert, thank you for your support in the early process of determining how to organize the Connect-to-Grow Approach. To Suzanne Kolb, Tracy Brown Hamilton, Rosie Colosi, and Leigh Anne Gardner for helping us figure out how to wrangle everything we are so passionate about that has informed Slumberkins into this book at different parts of the process. Finally, to Amy Fandrei at Wiley Publishing, thank you for seeing that it was time for us to bring all of this information, content, and context together for parents and for giving us this opportunity.

INTRODUCTION

Children who are encouraged to identify, understand, and regulate emotions experience wide-ranging, lifelong benefits including improved mental health and relationships. Our Connect-to-Grow approach—the foundation of Slumberkins—gives parents like you a way to apply proven therapeutic concepts in everyday moments to guide you in cultivating emotional wellness for your child, and ultimately yourself.

Just like you, we are tired parents who want to show up for our kids; we are always looking for ways to supercharge our existing routines so that there isn't necessarily more to do, but we're being more intentional when we do it. In this book, we'll help you find ways to meaningfully connect with your child that are easy for you and deeply impactful for them. We will give insights, tips, tools, and strategies that we've successfully used in schools and we try our best to also implement at home.

In many ways, our approach is less about *doing* and more about *being*. It focuses on guiding children—and in many cases parents—in understanding emotions and in caring for and expressing those emotions in a healthy way that leads to self-awareness and personal growth.

Because you are here reading this, we assume you are a parent or caregiver and you're interested in understanding the mental and emotional well-being of your child. You want them to be well adjusted and ready to handle whatever life may bring. This book may not be like other parenting books you've read before, however. We dive into the underlying beliefs that shape our self-concept and understanding of the world around us. We know that our early childhood experiences shape how we see the world, and we want to support you in being able to parent through all of the foundational years for your child. The effort you put in now will last a lifetime.

WHAT YOU WILL GET OUT OF THIS BOOK

This book will give you the tools and information you need to feel empowered to parent in a conscious way that supports your child's developing sense of self. It will help cultivate the skills, attitudes, and beliefs that will be with them through their entire life. It will also illuminate the process by which this happens and describe how you can support the healthy development of these vital capacities.

You will find strategies to help guide you through everyday moments to meet your child's emotional needs and support their emotional development. We hope that after applying some of these principles, you'll find that you'll be experiencing moments of connection that bring meaning and depth to your parenting that you didn't realize were so important.

The book is full of tips to help your child build these skills proactively, as well as strategies to help your child grow in a positive direction when times feel tough. We've blended and boiled down theories to make these practices accessible and family-friendly so that you can acknowledge and support your child's emotional needs on a deep level, from the infant stage through the tween years.

But we're not just here for your kids. We're here for you, too. This work may feel natural to some but overwhelming to others. Whichever side of the fence you land on, we want you to feel supported and informed on your journey as a parent.

HOW TO USE THIS BOOK

Anyone can implement this approach, whether you have experience with Slumberkins or Connect-to-Grow or not. We'll give you tangible, easy-to-implement tools that can take effect in just five minutes a day.

Part 1 of the book will give you the lay of the land. You'll learn more about how past parenting practices have led us to where we are now and the elements today's parents want to improve upon. You'll also discover the central tenets of the Connect-to-Grow approach and why and how you should use this approach with your family. You'll find ways to exercise this emotional muscle in your daily life and learn how maintaining this awareness will proactively help your kids to improve their emotional wellness. We are here to help you stay connected and feel confident in your ability to be the best parent you can be.

Part 2 is all about putting this approach into practice. You can work through the chapters in order, or you can prioritize the sections that encompass some of your child's more pressing struggles. Here, you'll find everyday situations that will benefit from more intentionality, as well as examinations of the tough stuff—situations we wish kids didn't have to experience. Each chapter explains the skill or theme we're focused on and gives you activities to implement to proactively build or show up when you need to support certain situations.

Because we completely understand the plight of a busy parent, we've designed this book so that you can choose your own adventure. You can start at the beginning and read straight through for the most in-depth overview of our approach, or you can cherry-pick your content based on your current family needs. There is a Use Case Guide at the end of the book for you to reference based on your needs.

Therapists are trained to meet you where you're at, and we want this book to function in the same way. We want to give you the tools to help with whatever is problematic in the moment in order to make the biggest impact, hoping that a first success will leave you open and available to keep trying to do this work.

—Kelly

ADDITIONAL FEATURES IN THE BOOK

Throughout the book, especially in Part 2, we include personal stories from us and a few of our collaborators that provide more context, specificity, and nuance in our approach. We hope these personal stories will better help you envision how Connect-to-Grow has worked in real-life situations, as well as illustrate that even educators or experts make mistakes and aren't always able to be what we know we should be when it comes to parenting. At the end of the day, we are two mothers trying our best, just like you. We make a conscious choice to show up and do this work, and we trust in the process and know the investment of time and emotional energy will pay off for our children and for future generations who will be that much more emotionally attuned.

You'll also notice that in Part 2 we introduce you to the mascots of the Slumberkins universe. They will be familiar to some readers and new to others. We do so to add a memorable (and adorable) face to each emotional skill and to point you in the right direction if you want to add these characters into your parenting routines.

PARENTS ARE THE EXPERTS ON THEIR CHILD'S EMOTIONAL HEALTH

Your child is part of your heart. They're part of your soul. There is no connection that's going to be stronger than their connection to you in this early childhood moment. And that can feel scary. . .but it's also beautiful.

Who better to teach them to tap into their emotions than you?

Kids are incredibly attuned to you and need to feel trust in you as their leader. You're the captain of your family ship; kids want to feel confident in the fact that you'll steer them in the right direction. However, no captain can run a ship alone. It's essential to surround yourself with a supportive crew to shoulder the mental load.

We're here to join your crew.

As much as I have learned and "know" the best way to handle these parenting moments, I am making mistakes every day, reflecting, repairing, and trying again. That's the whole point. There is no way to parent "perfectly." It's better to be present than perfect.

—Kelly

All Feelings Welcome

PART ONE

THE THEORY BEHIND THE CONNECT-TO-GROW APPROACH

CHAPTER 1

Early Emotional Learning Is Foundational

Early on in our educational careers, we were new moms working in education—and working on ourselves. We realized that our parents, and generations prior, didn't do much for our emotional wellness; instead they tried to manage our behavior.

When we were kids, there was a lot of "Go to your room if you're crying." There just wasn't support for emotional learning. It wasn't that our parents didn't want to support our emotional lives; they just didn't know they needed to.

Similarly, when we were in college learning to be educators, focus and importance were placed on being a good "classroom manager" and maintaining order among our students. The whole point of getting an education was to go to college to get a "good job," which were the same jobs that had existed for decades: doctor, lawyer, teacher. The learning process was all focused on achievement and rewards (and on shame if we didn't achieve those rewards). We learned techniques like using red/yellow/green behavior charts or sending a student to the principal's office as standard practice. Although these techniques are effective in the short term, we now understand that they can disrupt and harm the emotional development of a child. It can lead to children developing negative beliefs about themselves that stay with them long after they have left their school years behind them. What works in the short term is not best for our children in the long term.

Today, in the educational world, there has been a shift. The role of educators isn't necessarily to just get kids ready with the skills and knowledge they need to achieve but to help kids learn to be well-rounded, stable people who can go out into the world and find professional, emotional, and social success. Innovation is changing career options at a rapid pace— many of the jobs our kids may end up doing don't even exist yet. The skills they need are less about writing in cursive and doing math in a certain way—it's becoming more about navigating problem-solving, having a growth mindset, and being resilient.

Similarly, there has been a generational shift from equating "good behavior" with "good parenting." We are now raising our children in a more conscious way. We want to break old patterns by encouraging communication rather than punishment. This is not easy work, and takes a lot of effort, but the payoff is well worth it for everyone.

Having a child can really turn your world upside down. No matter how many siblings you have, kids you babysat, or books you read, adding another human being to your family will take some adjusting. When you have a child, it is a unique moment when you have the opportunity to reflect on life itself. You are naturally seeing yourself in new roles, reflecting on your own experiences in childhood, your parents, and your current situation. Life is inviting you into a new phase, and for those who jump in, excited to learn to be the best parent possible, you have an opportunity to grow and heal yourself right alongside your child. By reflecting on your own experience and trying to accept and support your child, you have an approach to interrupting the patterns that you experienced, giving your child the chance to grow up with increased emotional awareness.

Even as a well-educated, emotionally aware parent, you can easily fall into the trap of repeating patterns from your past. Particularly when you feel overwhelmed, finding the energy to address rather than punish or control a behavior can feel impossible. We know because we've been there. Stay the course and remember that your work can change your child's emotional life for the better.

I wouldn't be so passionate about sharing what I know as a family therapist if I didn't believe in everyone's capacity to change and grow at any moment in their lives. I've seen it happen with so many of my clients, families, and friends as they enter the parenting journey.

—Kelly

Improving your approach to emotional regulation can have far-reaching impacts. As a parent, you can truly support positive changes in the world through your relationships with your children. Those relationships begin with educating your child about their emotions so that they can learn from them. You don't want to "control" their emotions; instead, they should meet them with curiosity so they can be felt, expressed, and understood.

In this chapter, you will learn about the building blocks of the Connect-to-Grow approach so you can put emotional learning at the center of your experience.

THE MAGIC OF THE CONNECT-TO-GROW APPROACH

We know this approach works because we have personally seen and felt the magic that happens when we meaningfully connect and engage with our children routinely. We've also seen the benefits of this approach in the schools as educators with countless families over the years.

In simple words, Connect-to-Grow helps you meet your child's need to feel seen and heard. Sounds easy, right? Even taking just five minutes of intentional time with your child regularly leads to immeasurable benefits to the emotional health of your child. And those benefits may be felt immediately.

Regardless of what you have read or studied, becoming a parent shows us that *knowledge* and *lived experience* are very different things. Nothing quite prepares you for the highs and lows of the journey of parenting. You can read all the books in the months before the baby arrives. You can take all the classes. You might have younger siblings or worked as a nanny. But there's a major difference between *knowing* what you're supposed to do as a parent and actually *doing* it.

> Through my studies, I felt confident about becoming a parent because I had learned so much about family systems and therapeutic practices. When I actually became a parent, I realized that just because I knew what I should do, it didn't mean that I could actually do it in reality. Parenting smacked me in the face, saying "Nope! Just because you understand something doesn't mean that you're going to be able to do it any better than anybody else ever has."
>
> —Kelly

You can't fake your way through parenting. Your child is so attuned to you that they will feel and notice your emotional state, probably more than you would think possible. From an evolutionary perspective, a child's attachment to you is the way they survive. A child needs to be loved and connected to you in order to ensure their care. Because they are wired to connect on this deep level, whatever you are feeling internally can be and often subtly is felt by your child.

Once you understand and incorporate our approach with your child, you will see the magic is *you*. You have the power to make a meaningful impact for good in your child's formative years.

We hope that this roadmap will help you feel more confident and successful as a parent. When you start to see emotional maturity reflected back at you through your child, it makes the journey worthwhile. Imagine hearing your child reminding *you* that of course it's OK to make mistakes and that you are always lovable when you make mistakes. We will share some of our own examples of moments like this in Part 2, "Putting It into Practice."

WHERE DOES CONNECT-TO-GROW COME FROM?

As a teacher and as a school therapist, our expertise as educators lies in the therapeutic and social-emotional aspects of learning; we know that students won't be able to absorb new skills if they are not first emotionally regulated. Therapists are trained to support children and adults in not only identifying their emotions but knowing what those emotions suggest about their needs. Everyone wants to feel purpose in their life, and many times it is by understanding ourselves better that we find our path to meaningful experiences in adulthood. Understanding ourselves starts with investigating what lies beneath our emotions.

We approach things a bit differently. We have seen our peers grow up, go out into the world, and achieve—and yet their success isn't complete if they don't feel seen. Having a PhD or a high-paying job doesn't necessarily lead to happiness.

We want to set our kids up in a better way. We don't just want to help your children develop these skills so that they'll grow up to be a good scientist or a good mathematician (although those things are obviously useful!).

Instead, we think that emotional fluency is essential because it is your emotional world that paints your reality—how you view yourself in the world, how you view other people, and how you experience your full life. We give you a peek inside your child's emotional world, affirmations to help them develop a positive self-image, and actionable tips to help you support them at any age.

Connect-to-Grow goes beyond social-emotional learning by using everyday parenting situations and experiences to provide the awareness and structure around the formation of core beliefs, which are our deeply held understandings of the world around us. (We'll dive into those in Chapter 3, "Expanding on Core Beliefs.")

Our perspective is that children and caregivers often have what they need already inside of them. We've examined the research on how our brain works to process emotional content and information and how this processing of emotions impacts our functioning and relationships over time. We believe that when people are able to access the deep wisdom inside of themselves, they naturally move toward healing and growth when they can. Everyone has the capacity to grow and change.

The Connect-to-Grow approach has been influenced by the following:

- Carl Rogers (person-centered therapy)
- Garry Landreth (child-centered play therapy)
- Richard Schwartz (internal family systems theory)
- Dan Siegel (interpersonal neurobiology)
- Francine Shapiro (eye movement desensitization and reprocessing therapy)
- Stephen Porges (polyvagal theory)
- Erik Erikson (psychosocial development theory)
- Our own experiences as educators and moms

As we lay the groundwork for nurturing emotional and mental health and wellness in this part of the book, there is one trope that we must address. It is the source of much confusion around mental and emotional health that keeps us stuck in our patterns and unable to unlock the path to our own internal well-being. This trope has confined numerous well-intentioned people in internal prisons that might look good from the outside but *feel* constricting and hollow on the inside. It came from a good place but had some pretty limiting outcomes. It was what our parents wanted for us—an idea something along the lines of "I want my kids to be successful and happy."

Of course, this is a kind and wonderful sentiment. However, lurking under the surface of this wish are some unexplored assumptions that we think this generation has uncovered and is ready to break through.

First, success means nothing when you don't feel good inside.

What is success? Many of us assumed it was getting a good job, looking a certain way, and having the "right" things like the right shoes, house, car, or phone. Television, movies, social media, and even our neighbors showed us all the ways we could look the part, driving consumerism and outward displays of success. If we were *seen* as successful, then we *were* successful. Well, in actuality, people have started to admit that they don't feel fulfilled by this kind of success. Just looking the part isn't eliciting the internal feeling of satisfaction that we had hoped. We want to feel successful because we are in alignment with our purpose. But many of us didn't even know where to start. We have been told what success looks like, and if we don't see that success reflected back at us, we feel like we have failed.

Second, happiness is a feeling; it is not a goal, a destination, or a state that one can live in at all times.

Many of us believed from the stories we read or the movies we watched that we would live happily ever after once we reached our goals. Except, those stories never really showed us *how* to do that. Once we thought we reached our happily ever after, we discovered that we were *not* happy the whole time. In fact, we had a lot of other feelings—feelings that we assumed were not "good feelings" like happiness but "bad feelings" like anger, loneliness, or jealousy. When we assume that we are only supposed to feel good feelings, we would again feel like failures if we felt bad feelings. We needed to find ways to shut down those bad feelings.

We want to offer a new direction for our kids. We want our children to be caring, confident, and resilient—prepared for anything life throws their way. We want them to find their purpose, live it, and feel fulfilled, aligned, and well. To build the roadmap to those goals, we must all agree and be open to the idea that all feelings are welcome.

ALL FEELINGS ARE WELCOME

There are no "bad feelings" or inherently "good feelings." Feelings are morally neutral messengers. They are the language of our inner world, showing us our needs, fears, and hurts at any given moment. Our minds make meaning out of feelings very quickly, but every feeling has a deeper message. Sometimes feelings tell us about a need, and sometimes feelings are just energy being processed and moving through our bodies. When we can truly welcome all of our feelings, we find our way to become in alignment with our deepest truths and our connection to Self and others. When we hold space and openness for whatever messages we receive from our feelings, we start to become aware of our programming. We are able to consciously choose where to direct our attention and focus on the fulfillment of our lives. It gives us the freedom to live with emotional wellness.

We certainly hope this book helps you welcome your own feelings, as well as your child's, in order to grow into a more aligned, fulfilled human. But if nothing else, we hope that this book helps you understand the stages of early emotional learning occurring in—and between—you and your child. You may find some parts intuitive, while you need other sections explained a bit more so you can understand them on a deeper level. We find that having the context of *why* something is important and *how* to use it works best to help you incorporate these ideas in your everyday life. Once you have that deeper understanding of the *why* behind your child's actions (and your reactions), you'll be able to better handle parenting situations that come your way with a whole new set of tools at your disposal.

CHAPTER 2

Stages of Emotional Development

As you can imagine, children undergo an extended and complex amount of learning in their formative years. The amount of information they process during that time would feel unfathomable to us as adults. You, as a primary caregiver, are there to guide them on their journey, and the relationship that they have with you can shape how they move through the world for the rest of their lives. They will follow your lead, so it's important for you to lead them in the right direction. You are their Mr. Miyagi, their Yoda, their Dumbledore, their wise leader who helps them learn and grow and discover.

Forming a secure bond with our children is the most important thing you can do as a parent or caregiver, and parents have a much easier time forming that bond when they understand where children are at in terms of emotional development. In the past, only therapists or counselors were aware of a child's stages of emotional development so they could be helpful if "issues" arose. However, we think that information is valuable to parents so you can use it to deepen your relationship and help your child grow. In this chapter, we'll present a fresh look at the important stages and what you need to know about each one as you learn to take the lead on your child's emotional development.

ATTACHMENT RELATIONSHIPS

Our approach focuses on moments between you and your child that support healthy bonds. Those moments can be as simple as diapering and feeding your baby, gazing into their eyes and smiling as they fall asleep in your arms, playing peek-a-boo, or supporting them through a meltdown or tantrum. To make these moments meaningful, intentionally meet these basic needs in a way that is stable, consistent, and attuned. When practiced, these moments help create a secure relationship between you and your child, giving them the framework for how they will understand themselves and the world around them. It's astounding how many of their future choices, viewpoints, beliefs, and situations are impacted by their relationship with you.

By focusing on the quality of your relationship with your child, you can support their ability to become more loving, empathetic, well-rounded, and emotionally in-tune adults. The hope is that they will become loving, empathetic, well-rounded, emotionally in-tune adults.

Your relationship with your child is known as a *primary attachment relationship*. In essence, it is the first love relationship they experience, and it gives your child the framework for defining love in a larger context throughout their life. It is the lens through which they see the world. It informs how worthy they feel of love, safety, and connection.

An infant generally learns that when they cry, a caregiver will come and help them. That develops into the understanding that they can ask for help and will receive a response in a host of other instances. Kindergarteners with positive attachment relationships know that if they scrape their knee, their primary caregiver may provide a bandage and a kiss. Teenagers learn that even if they give you an intense attitude because they want to hang out with friends rather than going on a family vacation, you'll still be there for them when they decide to give in and have fun with the family. Adults know that if everything in life seems to go wrong, they can ask for help and find a way through. When they have had the comfort of being cared for since infanthood, they believe that someone will show up for them if they're in a bind.

Attachment relationships also come into play in future intimate relationships. By establishing a secure attachment relationship with our children, we're not just improving our relationship with them. We're also giving them "relationship vitamins" to help their future pairings grow strong. There is some truth to the fact that some people "marry their father." Many psychologists and therapists will say that the unconscious patterns created by our attachments often drive our attachments to our partners. Therefore, we often re-create the same patterns or issues that we felt during childhood in our adult romantic relationships. So we may, in fact, select a partner who reminds us of one of our own parents, even if we don't consciously realize it. Essentially, this is another opportunity to engage in healing and self-awareness through an important loving relationship. Though in childhood you "get what you get," adults are ideally able to consciously create the kind of loving connection they need to feel whole.

Given the enormous impact of primary attachment relationships, it may feel a bit daunting to do this "right" as a parent. But don't worry. Even if you feel that you have done things "wrong" or are worried about the future, there are always ways to support and improve your connection. Everyone's emotional journey can begin right where they are. Just by loving your child, you are making a positive impact on their lives. But by adding some awareness to the process, you can truly give them resources and tools to empower themselves to move through the world in an emotionally aware way.

Our goal is for you to develop a "secure" attachment relationship with your child. But to achieve that goal, you first have to examine the different types of attachment relationships. You may recognize some of these in your life. There's no need to try to "diagnose" yourself or your child; rather, this research explains the foundation of our approach.

In the field of child development, our understanding of attachment styles has been profoundly shaped by the pioneering research of developmental psychologist Mary Ainsworth and psychiatrist John Bowlby. They laid the groundwork for identifying the various ways children form emotional bonds and attachments to their caregivers. The following are tangible examples of the four attachment styles—secure, anxious-preoccupied, dismissive-avoidant, and disorganized—as outlined in their research. Many times, we have a mix of these styles or characteristics of different attachment styles. Understanding these attachment styles provides interesting and invaluable insights into the emotional world of children.

Secure attachment: Children with a secure attachment often show confidence in their caregiver's availability and responsiveness.

Example: A child who comfortably explores new environments but regularly checks back with their parent, or who is comfortable and quickly reassured when a parent returns after a brief absence, demonstrates secure attachment. These children openly express their needs and are easily comforted, reflecting the healthy, responsive bond they share with their caregivers.

Anxious-preoccupied attachment: Children who exhibit an anxious-preoccupied attachment style display high levels of dependency and require constant reassurance.

Example: A child who becomes extremely distressed when a caregiver leaves and isn't easily soothed upon return demonstrates an anxious-preoccupied attachment. They might cling excessively and demonstrate reluctance to engage in independent play, showing their heightened anxiety about the caregiver's availability.

Dismissive-avoidant attachment: Children who exhibit the dismissive-avoidant attachment style might appear emotionally distant and overly independent.

Example: A child who doesn't actively seek contact or comfort from caregivers, appears indifferent to their comings and goings, and is self-reliant in play exemplifies dismissive-avoidant attachment. This often results from a caregiver's consistent unresponsiveness or dismissiveness to the child's emotional needs.

Disorganized attachment: Children who exhibit this attachment style are characterized by inconsistent and contradictory behaviors.

Example: A child who shows a mix of avoidant and anxious behaviors may approach the caregiver but exhibit an inability to engage meaningfully or may appear disoriented upon a caregiver's return. These behaviors often reflect the child's confusion and lack of a coherent strategy to manage their attachment needs.

It's crucial for parents to recognize that these styles are not static; they are fluid and can evolve with changes in the child's environment and the caregiver's responsiveness. When you move toward parenting approaches to meet your child's unique emotional needs, you can foster a more secure and healthy attachment, paving the way for their emotional resilience and well-being. Recognizing and adapting to your child's attachment style can significantly enhance the quality of your relationship, ensuring a strong foundation for their emotional development and future relationships. In a nutshell, secure attachments matter.

Throughout this book, we will help you support your child, but we are also committed to supporting you as a whole person. Identifying your own attachment style can be a deeply insightful process, shedding light on how you form and maintain relationships. Here are five reflective questions to help you explore and identify your attachment style:

How do I respond to intimacy and closeness in my relationships? Reflect on your comfort level with emotional intimacy. Do you embrace closeness and feel comfortable sharing your innermost thoughts and feelings, or do you tend to keep part of yourself reserved? Do you find yourself craving more intimacy than your relationships provide, or do you prefer to maintain a sense of independence and distance?

What is my typical reaction to a partner's or close friend's need for space or independence? Consider how you feel when someone close to you wants to spend time apart or pursue their interests independently. Are you supportive and understanding, anxious and worried, or indifferent and detached?

How do I handle conflict in relationships? Think about your approach to resolving disagreements or conflicts. Do you address issues openly and work toward a solution, or do you tend to avoid confrontations? Do you find conflicts deeply unsettling to the point where they make you question the entire relationship, or do you view them as a normal part of relating to others?

What are my expectations from relationships, and how do I react when they are not met? Reflect on what you expect from close relationships and how you cope when your expectations are unmet. Do you feel secure and able to adjust your expectations, or do you experience significant distress? Do your unmet expectations lead you to question your worth or the value of the relationship?

How do I view and respond to emotional needs—both mine and those of others? Consider your comfort level in expressing your emotional needs and how you respond when others express theirs. Are you empathetic and responsive, or do you find it challenging to deal with emotions, whether your own or those of others?

Your responses to the questions about attachment styles can provide significant clues about which category you might fall into. Here's a basic guide to interpreting your responses:

Secure attachment: If you find yourself comfortable with intimacy and closeness and can maintain your independence without feeling threatened or overwhelmed, you likely lean toward a secure attachment style. You handle conflict constructively, viewing it as an opportunity for growth rather than a threat. You're generally supportive when your partner or friend needs space, and you express your needs and feelings openly and respectfully.

Anxious-preoccupied attachment: If you often worry about your relationships, feel that you want more intimacy than your partner or friend is willing to give, or frequently fear being abandoned or rejected, you might have an anxious-preoccupied attachment style. You may find conflict deeply unsettling, possibly worrying it could lead to the end of the relationship. You might struggle when a partner or friend needs space, feeling insecure or neglected.

Dismissive-avoidant attachment: If you highly value independence in relationships, often feel that others are trying to get too close, or prefer not to depend on others or have others depend on you, you may have a dismissive-avoidant attachment style. You might avoid deep emotional connections and downplay the importance of relationships. During conflicts, you might withdraw and prefer to deal with issues independently.

Fearful-avoidant (disorganized) attachment: If you find yourself wanting close relationships but struggle with trusting others or if you experience mixed feelings about intimacy, swinging between needing it and fearing it, you might exhibit a fearful-avoidant (disorganized) attachment style. You might react unpredictably to conflict and have difficulty articulating your needs or responding to the needs of others.

Relationships might feel very turbulent, and you might simultaneously desire closeness and distance.

Remember, these are simplified interpretations, and human emotions and relationships are complex. People may exhibit traits from different styles, and attachment styles can evolve over time with self-awareness and personal growth. If you're interested in exploring your attachment style further, it might be helpful to consult a therapist or counselor who can provide more nuanced and personalized insights.

Regardless of the attachment style we grew up with, we can learn new skills and have different experiences that help us rewire our brain and nervous system and move into secure attachments with our kids, partners, family, or close friends. We call this rewiring process "the work." There's no set amount of time it takes to see the difference in your relationships, but change will come. There's no end, no finish line. Just a continued deepening of your emotional bond.

Through this book, we are examining the emotional side of who your child is becoming, looking at who you're becoming through being a parent, and trying to supercharge both of those things with support and tools that you can easily pick up as you encounter future roadblocks (like the first day of daycare or the first time your child gets teased by another child).

If you're already aware of the Slumberkins characters and world, then you may recognize that all of our books and content are simply tools—shortcuts or affirmations—to give you the words and actions that will build positive skills or help you show up in tough moments. But with or without implementing Slumberkins stories or content, there are everyday moments that you can capitalize on to build secure, positive attachment relationships with your child.

For example:

- When your child wakes up in the morning and you have cuddle time
- When you drop them off at school and make eye contact and give them a hug goodbye

- When you hand them their favorite snack in the car and tell them you bought that particular snack because you know how much they like it

All of these actions are moments when attachment happens naturally. Words, however, have complementary power, and they can add to the presence and connection you are having with your child. These are some examples of phrases that might highlight attachment:

- "I want to be there with you."
- "I love you."
- "I want to take care of you."
- "You make me happy."
- "I want to snuggle and kiss you."

If you experienced a secure attachment in one way or another, all of the these phrases may feel completely natural to you. But some people missed these moments as a child, and they may not feel as natural. Saying them may require a bit more work.

For all the times you've felt those loving moments that contribute to building secure attachment, you have most likely also experienced pain, disconnection, and disappointment. Attachment connections are not just about the connected times but about how we come back into connection after moments of disconnection. They are inextricably linked.

Just remember that even the best parents will inevitably disappoint or disconnect from their children. There is no perfect way to always remain in connection. These are some of the ways we are guilty of those moments:

- Texting when our kids are trying to talk to us
- Forgetting to pick them up from school on an early-release day
- Saying no when our kids ask us to play with them even though we don't have something important to do

The "dance" of our roles as parents as we connect, disconnect, and re-engage with our children sets the stage for our attachment relationship style. Many of us have mixed attachment styles in varying degrees, because of the meaning that we made of that dance as a child.

At each stage, children focus on a different aspect of emotional development. Let's take a closer look at their potential for learning at each stage.

WHAT'S HAPPENING IN EACH STAGE AND HOW OUR EMOTIONAL WORLD IS SHAPED

The stages of social-emotional learning as we know them today were pioneered by the early works of Erik Erikson. We're going to describe these stages, which are widely cited and studied, because they underpin many modern therapeutic and educational practices that have influenced us. Each stage is deeply influenced by the environment, biology (genetics), and relationships.

ERIKSON'S STAGES OF PSYCHOSOCIAL DEVELOPMENT THROUGH AGE 13

APPROXIMATE AGE	PSYCHOSOCIAL CRISIS/TASK	VIRTUE DEVELOPED
Infant–18 months	Trust vs Mistrust	Hope
18 months–3 years	Autonomy vs Shame/Doubt	Will
3–5 years	Initiative vs Guilt	Purpose
5–13 years	Industry vs Inferiority	Competency

We studied Erikson's work and applied his view of developmental stages to our approach to building positive core beliefs throughout a child's life. It is essential to seek positive outcomes at each stage because Erikson believed that an incomplete or negative outcome would likely impact future stages of development. We have seen and experienced for ourselves how core beliefs have impacted our own struggles and repeated patterns in our lives, and we want to set our kids up for something different.

One of our professors used to say that we are the generation of the "walking well." He meant there are many people who have had a "good childhood." They appear to be fine and function well in society, but they have a significant amount of emotional healing left to accomplish that would improve their life significantly. We believe that by understanding the stages, we can see how we might have picked up messages that have impacted us throughout a lifetime. If we can recognize that in ourselves, we can try to be aware of our own children's development to help them consciously form positive core beliefs.

Let's walk through the stages of social-emotional development that apply to early emotional learning. Identifying the stage of development your child is at will help you understand what sort of understanding they may be building about themselves and the world at any given time in their emotional development.

EMOTIONAL MILESTONES + CORE BELIEF CONNECTIONS

AGE	EMOTIONAL SKILL	STRENGTH	CORE BELIEF CONNECTION
BABY Infant–18 months	Trust	Hope	I am connected I am important I am safe
TODDLER 18 months–3 years	Autonomy	Will	I am lovable I am seen I am good enough just the way I am
LITTLE KIDS 3–5 years	Initiative	Purpose	I am capable I am worthy of love and connection I can get help when I need it
BIG KIDS 5–13 years	Abilities	Competence	I know what I like I can recognize what I can and cannot control I have inner strength

Emotional Milestones + Core Belief Connections

If children move into a new age without successfully understanding the emotional skill necessary to build upon, they can carry forward negative beliefs, or ways of functioning, that impact their future developmental learning. Lagging emotional skills can cause and shape negative core beliefs within each milestone; those beliefs need to be resolved and healed in order to continuously build the positive foundation within us. This is why we say that emotional development can begin at any age. Even though the number of years we've been on earth continues marching forward, our emotional path can leap forward, skip a skill, or circle back to the beginning. It's not a straight path.

Understanding the core beliefs that children might be forming at different stages of Erikson's psychosocial development is crucial for parents. Here's how you can help your children navigate these stages.

Stage 1: Can I Trust the World?

Babies (Infant–18 Months)

POSITIVE BELIEFS:
- "I am safe."
- "I am valued."
- "My needs are important."

HOW TO NURTURE:
- Consistently respond to your infant's needs.
- Provide comfort, nourishment, and affection.
- A consistent and loving response helps build a sense of security and trust.

AVOID NEGATIVE BELIEFS:
- Inconsistent or neglectful responses can lead to beliefs like "I am not important" or "The world is not safe."
- Ensure the infant feels loved and cared for.

You may think that the daily life of a newborn isn't that dynamic since prevailing conversation mostly centers around how they eat, sleep, and poop. But in fact, 90% of the brain is formed during this period, and it sets the foundation for all the stages to come. Those little minds are doing a lot of deep internal work.

Because children are so dependent on their caregivers in this stage, meeting physical and emotional needs is critical. We do this by responding to their cries, feeding them, and changing their diapers. When we do this in an attuned manner, it creates the building blocks for emotional growth and development. Attunement, in practical terms, involves focusing on your child's emotional state and responding in a way that lets them know they are understood, valued, and important. It's about creating a "dance" of emotional interaction that helps you and your baby find the same rhythm.

For instance, when your baby coos or makes sounds, try mimicking these sounds back to them. This simple action not only delights your baby but also teaches them the basics of communication and interaction. It's as if you're having your very first "conversations" with your baby; their sounds and your responses help build a deep connection.

You can also demonstrate emotional attunement by recognizing and responding to your baby's cries. Each cry can signal different needs or discomforts. By trying to understand these subtle differences and responding appropriately—whether it's time for feeding, a diaper change, or just some cuddling—you are showing your baby that their needs are being heard and met. This responsiveness builds trust, a crucial component of a secure attachment.

Physical touch—gentle, loving caresses, cuddles, and snuggles—provide a sense of security and comfort. These actions reassure your infant that they are safe and loved, which is essential for their emotional development. Engaging in gentle tickles or simple games like peek-a-boo encourages joyful interactions.

In quieter moments, like bedtime, attuning to your baby can be as simple as maintaining eye contact, softly singing a lullaby, or gently rocking them. These soothing activities create a peaceful environment that reinforces a sense of safety and love.

When the Newborn Phase Doesn't Feel "Easy" or Natural   We believe that babies are whole people and deserve the same respect and connection you would give to an adult. Your job isn't to form them into something; your job is to give them all the tools to help them navigate the world themselves and be in alignment with themselves.

That means you can have boundaries, even with babies.

While we are striving to help meet their needs, we are also supporting them in learning how to self-soothe; gradually, they will learn to meet some of their own needs. Especially in those overwhelming moments, it is OK to feel this way and even tell your baby this. Maybe that looks like saying "I hear you are upset and want to be picked up right now, but Mommy is going to finish her breakfast first. Then I will pick you up." You don't want your child to scream at top volume for 20 minutes at a time, but you also don't have to respond immediately. Even if they don't understand your words yet, they will understand your tone. Remember to take care of yourself and balance your baby's needs with your own.

Self-Care: Essential for Both You and Your Baby   If you want to take good care of others, you must take good care of yourself. Let's look at the different ways you can meet your own self-care needs, especially in the early stages of parenting, because sometimes a bubble bath just won't cut it.

Physical Self-Care   Taking care of your body is essential for maintaining the energy and health needed to care for your child. Simple activities such as ensuring adequate sleep, eating nutritious meals, and engaging in gentle exercises, like walking or yoga, can significantly impact your physical well-being. Remember, a healthy body supports a healthy mind.

Emotional Self-Care   Acknowledging and addressing your emotional needs is key to preventing burnout and maintaining a positive mental state. It's OK to seek support, whether through talking with friends, joining a parenting group, or seeking professional help if needed. Practices such as journaling or meditation can also be valuable tools for managing stress and emotional upheaval.

Social Self-Care   Maintaining social connections is crucial, even in the whirlwind of new parenthood. Stay in touch with friends, family, or fellow parents. Even brief interactions can provide support, a fresh perspective, and a much-needed sense of belonging and normalcy. On the other hand, if you need to say no because you're approaching burnout and need more time to yourself, set that boundary and don't be afraid to say no.

Intellectual Self-Care   Keeping your mind engaged and stimulated is just as important as caring for your emotional and physical health. Find time for activities that stimulate your mind—reading, engaging in a hobby, or even watching a thought-provoking show. These activities can provide a refreshing break from the routine of childcare.

Spiritual Self-Care   Spiritual self-care involves activities that nourish your soul and bring deeper meaning or connection to your life, like meditation, prayer, spending time in nature, or any practice that helps you feel connected to either your inner self or a larger purpose.

Self-Reflection: Understanding Your Own Journey   Equally important in the realm of self-care is self-reflection—understanding your own attachment style and how it influences your parenting. Reflect on your childhood and consider how your experiences with your caregivers have shaped your beliefs and behaviors. This understanding can illuminate your parenting journey, helping you to replicate positive aspects and change patterns you don't want to continue. Consider journaling about your hopes and beliefs for your parenting journey. What values do you want to instill in your child? What aspects of your own upbringing do you want to emulate or avoid? Reflecting on these questions can provide clarity and purpose in your daily parenting decisions.

Community   For parents, community is everything. In the early years, infants directly benefit from the support that their caregivers receive from the community. It is through a sense of belonging, connection, encouragement, inspiration, and support that we get anything done. The world is not meant for individuals to survive alone, and that's why we want everyone to bring their unique gifts and perspectives to the whole. Any opportunity to create community, to connect with people in a deeper way, to grow ourselves, to learn, to be supported, and to support others is going to lift us all up.

Think back to that terrifying moment when the nurses at the hospital placed your baby in your arms and helped you into your car. You might have started the car, turned to your parenting partner, and thought, "We have no idea what we're doing." If you were on your own from that moment on, parenthood would be a terrifying experience.

But maybe your mom was waiting at your house to help bring the baby inside and told you to take a nap. Maybe you called your sister crying at 4 a.m. because the baby just wouldn't sleep and she calmed you down. Maybe you posted panicked questions about local daycares in your neighborhood parent group chat and received well-informed, reassuring feedback. Family, friends, neighbors, and parents you've only communicated with online—they're all part of different communities that can provide cheerleading and advice.

It takes a village to raise a child, but these days, the village can look a lot different than it used to. Community can be found online in parent groups on social media, connecting us across the world with other parents in the same stage of life, going through the same struggles. Or, it can be found in your best friend or partner coming over just to sit next to you in the chaos and letting you take a minute for yourself. Or maybe it's your parents, engaging your five-year-old in a video chat so you can make dinner in peace. However you find community, you will benefit enormously. Community helps us feel connected, secure, and supported.

Stage 2: Is It OK to Be Me?

Toddler (18 Months–3 Years)

POSITIVE CORE BELIEFS:
- "I am capable."
- "I can do things myself."
- "It's OK to be independent."

HOW TO NURTURE:
- Encourage exploration and allow your toddler to try tasks on their own, like dressing themselves or choosing their snack.
- Offer guidance without taking over.

AVOIDING NEGATIVE BELIEFS:
- Overprotection or criticism can lead to beliefs like "I am not capable" or "I can't do anything right."
- Offer support and celebrate their efforts.

In this exciting phase of growth, your little one is embarking on a journey of self-discovery. Your infant who was fully dependent on you has now become a toddler who starts to assert their independence, testing their abilities and exploring the world in their own unique way. They explore their environment, discovering the most fascinating things, like electrical outlets, old gum stuck to the sidewalk, or the valuable antiques your parents like to keep on their coffee table. As anyone who has ever spent time with a toddler knows, this phase can be exhausting for caregivers who want to keep their child safe from harm as they adventure out into the world and further from your arms.

At the heart of this stage is the balance between developing autonomy and overcoming any feelings of shame and doubt. They learn that, for better or worse, they are their own person, separate from you. It's all about helping your child feel capable and confident in their newfound independence. As a parent, this means supporting their efforts to do things on their own. Yes, this might mean more time spent on tasks or a little extra mess—like when they insist on feeding themselves or choosing their own outfits (farewell, matching sets!). But the confidence they gain is priceless.

Potty training is a classic milestone during this time. More than just a transition out of diapers, it's a significant step in emotional development. It's about building self-assurance and independence, something that will serve them well in the future.

Navigating this stage involves setting boundaries while also understanding the emotional cues you're giving to your child. It's a balancing act: too few limits and discipline becomes shaky; too many limits and you risk instilling doubt and shame. There's no universal method here; you need to tune in to your child's needs and your own parenting style, which is easier said than done.

It can be difficult to serve your own needs *and* the needs of your child in this stage. For instance, imagine your child roars like a dinosaur during your important phone call. It's natural to ask them to be quiet. However, these moments are delicate; they can affect how your child sees themselves. After your call, why not explore their dinosaur world with them? We still hold the boundary and make sure that we take care of our needs (like having quiet during phone calls), but finding times when we can join them in their world is also important. Does this mean you need to do this every time you set a limit? No. It means it's something to be aware of and try to find ways to balance the scale.

If you find yourself shushing or chastising your child constantly without trying to find opportunity to connect with them on their level, they might think, "Mommy got upset when I was loud. Does she love me less when I'm noisy?" On days or seasons when you set strict boundaries, make sure you also leave time to read an extra book at bedtime or play pretend for a little longer than you usually do. It's in these everyday interactions that we have the chance to reinforce our unconditional love and acceptance in ways that are aligned developmentally with our child.

PARENT PERSPECTIVE

Remember, self-awareness is key. As you guide your child through this phase, it's also a time for your own growth. Many of us will find aspects of our own childhood resurfacing, which offers a chance for healing and understanding alongside our children. For example, if your child roars like a dinosaur during your important phone call, your mind may flash to a time in your childhood when you were lonely when your mother took on extra shifts at work or when you had a babysitter who ignored you. You'll have a chance to work through those memories and experiences of your own as you help your child navigate their own personal growth.

In essence, this stage is about nurturing your child's sense of self and providing the right mix of freedom and guidance. It's about understanding that each messy, independent choice they make is a step toward their self-confidence. And as you lovingly guide them, remember that the way you respond and connect in these small moments has a big impact on their developing sense of self. You're not just managing a little person asserting "I can do it"; you're shaping a future adult who believes in their own capabilities.

Stage 3: Is It OK for Me to Try New Things?

Little Kid (3–5 Years)

POSITIVE CORE BELIEFS:
- "I can make good things happen."
- "My ideas are valuable."

HOW TO NURTURE:
- Encourage imaginative play and creativity.
- Support their ideas and initiatives, even if they seem trivial or unrealistic.

AVOIDING NEGATIVE BELIEFS:
- Dismissing their ideas or overly punishing mistakes can lead to beliefs like "My ideas are not important" or "I am bad."
- Encourage kids to express themselves and explore.

Welcome to a vibrant stage in your child's development, in which imagination and reality weave a fascinating tapestry in their growing minds. This is the age of initiative, a time when your child's social awareness blossoms and they begin to ask the big *why* questions about the world around them. *Why is the sky blue? Why can't babies take care of themselves? Why can't I eat pancakes all the time?*

After exploring their physical abilities, your child now turns their curiosity outward, eager to understand how they fit into the wider world. It's a magical time when their imagination knows no bounds. You might find your three-year-old chatting away with an imaginary friend or your four-year-old puzzled about why they can't soar like a bird. These are not just whimsical thoughts; they are vital steps in your child's cognitive and emotional development. During this phase, the line between fantasy and reality is delightfully blurred for your child. This is a natural and essential part of their growth. It's through these imaginative explorations that they start to understand complex concepts like empathy, cause and effect, and the nuances of social interactions.

This is also a period where children start to form a self-concept based on their interactions and experiences. They often think in terms of "good" or "bad." *Am I a good kid or a bad kid?* Your responses and guidance are crucial here. Reinforce the idea that your child is innately good inside, no matter what. When it comes to *who* your child is as a person, "good" and "bad" do not apply.

Social skills take a front seat during these years. Playdates, preschool, and family gatherings become arenas for your child to learn about friendship, sharing, cooperation, and, sometimes, conflict resolution. Encourage these interactions, but also be there to guide and support them as they navigate the complexities of building relationships.

These social events may be stressful to you, since your child likely hasn't mastered the art of taking turns or saying a polite "No, thank you" when offered unfamiliar food. As their shouts of "MINE!" or "YUCK!" echo throughout the fancy restaurant at your parents' anniversary dinner, you might feel discouraged, as though you are a "bad" parent. Remember to give yourself the same grace you give your child. Chances are that the majority of people you come into contact with either have been in the same position themselves or will lend you their silent support in your battle with an overtired two-year-old. Positive reinforcement, patience, and open communication will help your child develop healthy self-esteem.

PARENT PERSPECTIVE

Your role is to provide a safe and nurturing environment for your child's exploration. Encourage their imaginative play, and join in their wonder. We know that sitting down on the floor to play pretend might not be your top priority when you arrive home after a long day at work, but throwing yourself wholeheartedly into just five or ten minutes of uninterrupted play can benefit both you and your child greatly.

When they ask questions like "Why can't I fly like a bird?" engage with their curiosity. Explore the answers together, nurturing a love for learning and discovery. This is not just about answering questions but about fostering an inquisitive mind.

Stage 4: What Can I Bring to the World?

> ### Big Kid (5–13 Years)
>
> **POSITIVE CORE BELIEFS:**
> - "I am competent."
> - "I can succeed."
>
> **HOW TO NURTURE:**
> - Encourage their interests and efforts in school, sports, arts, or other activities.
> - Celebrate their achievements and provide constructive feedback.
>
> **AVOIDING NEGATIVE BELIEFS:**
> - Comparison with others or focusing only on failures can lead to beliefs like "I am not good enough" or "I always fail."
> - Focus on their personal growth and strengths.

As your child steps into the school-age years, they embark on a new chapter filled with learning, competition, and deepening social connections. This stage, often beginning around five years old, is marked by a noticeable shift in focus toward academic achievements, friendships, and peer dynamics. As children move from their home environment to a school environment, their teacher becomes a "secondary primary caregiver." The relationship your child has with their teachers in their early school experiences are very important for their emotional development as well. You have planted the seeds, and the teacher will be watering and tending the garden now.

In this phase, the importance of social feedback escalates. Your child's self-esteem and confidence can be significantly influenced by their successes and challenges in school and social settings. It's crucial to recognize that struggles in these areas can stem from earlier developmental experiences. For instance, a child who hasn't fully embraced their autonomy in earlier stages may find it challenging to take initiative in school tasks or may overly rely on adult assistance. Conversely, some children may develop a strong need for perfection, constantly striving to meet high standards that can lead to stress or anxiety.

One key aspect of navigating this stage effectively is fostering a healthy balance between achievement and well-being. Encourage your child to strive for their best but also teach them that their value isn't solely defined by grades or wins. Help them understand that mistakes and failures are natural and valuable parts of learning. Additionally, this is a crucial time to cultivate social skills and empathy. Encourage your child to make friends, understand different viewpoints, and develop compassion. Activities like team sports, group projects, and family discussions about feelings and perspectives can be incredibly beneficial.

This stage is also where your child's understanding of the world, formed in the safety of your home, is put to the test. Children will encounter diverse perspectives and ideas, learning to navigate relationships beyond the family. It's a time when the stories they've come to believe about themselves are challenged and new narratives begin to form. These narratives can significantly influence their self-perception into adulthood.

PARENT PERSPECTIVE

As a parent, your role evolves in this stage. While you continue to provide love and support, encouraging independence becomes increasingly important. This means trusting your child to make decisions, solve problems, and navigate their social world, while still being there to guide and support them. It can feel supremely difficult to shoo your child out into the world while desperately wanting to keep them safe from every bit of potential harm, but part of your role is to make sure your kids have the ability to exist independently of you. It can feel daunting to let go, so remind your child (and yourself!) that you will always be there to catch them if they stumble.

Throughout these four early stages of emotional development, it's important for you to be aware of your own responses and attitudes. Children are highly perceptive and often internalize the emotional and behavioral cues of their caregivers. By providing a supportive, understanding, and nurturing environment, you can significantly influence the formation of positive core beliefs in your children, laying a foundation for healthy emotional and psychological development.

We know that you want to foster a secure, confident, and independent young person while nurturing your growth as an empathetic and understanding parent, and we're here to help you accomplish both of those goals. Remember, in the world of parenting, every challenge is also an opportunity for growth, both for you and your child.

CHAPTER 3

Expanding on Core Beliefs

ore beliefs are the lens through which we experience the world around us. They are our most deeply held beliefs about ourselves, others, and the world. Since core beliefs are learned in childhood, we have an excellent opportunity to set our children up for success by teaching them about core beliefs early on, making sure that the stories they tell themselves are positive, flexible ones.

As humans, we have always understood other people and the world around us by telling ourselves stories. Think about the family memories you probably share around the dinner table in story form, like that time you got poison ivy and gave it to everyone in your extended family or when you "accidentally" cut your little brother's hair the day before school pictures were scheduled. The stories we tell are often based on our lived experiences, and we hold on to those stories. Over time, the stories can stray from the truth, but they *seem* true.

We tell stories about ourselves, too. The stories that we tell ourselves in childhood are fairly simple and lack the complex perspective we have as adults. But because these stories started in the early stages of our emotional development, they can become core beliefs and linger all the way through our adult lives.

To illustrate how these beliefs form, we'll share some of our own negative core beliefs, plus insights we've gained from becoming aware of the patterns that developed as we grew into adulthood.

CALLIE'S STORY

I am a very independent person, sometimes to a fault. I tend to think that if I don't do what needs to be done, no one will. I'd rather just take on the extra stress or mental load instead of asking for help and being disappointed in a lack of response or someone else's inability to support me after I vocalize a need.

This is an example of a pattern and way of functioning from a negative core belief that formed from childhood; it has followed me into adulthood and impacted my relationships. To set the stage for how this negative core belief developed, it's helpful to share some background and context.

I'm an only child. My parents had me as older parents. I knew I was loved, and I was the apple of their eye—they often called me their miracle baby. Everything they did was centered around me, to make my life better. They're very kind, faithful, and loving parents. They both worked for Nabisco, where overtime shifts fueled the ability to give me every opportunity to open doors for any experience they wanted me to have.

Functioning this way also meant they were tired and exhausted (who wouldn't be?), and I formed a belief somewhere over the years that if I wanted something, I just needed to take care of it on my own. As a child, because my parents were working or sleeping after a night shift, I was alone a lot. Even if a parent was physically present and I knew I could wake them up and ask for help if I needed to, I was on my own. I figured it out. I watched a lot of *The Price Is Right* and *Matlock* during summer breaks and lived off cinnamon-sugar toast and ramen noodles. (This wasn't always the norm—we did have nights of family dinners, too!)

And spoiler alert: I did get a basketball scholarship for college thanks to them providing me with the opportunity to play on very expensive club travel teams, which exposed me to college coaches and recruiters.

Now, though, through doing the work and trying to understand my pattern of taking on too much, feeling vulnerable when I need to ask for help, and years of overfunctioning, I can identify that my experience through childhood eventually accumulated to form some negative core beliefs, like these:

"I am on my own."
"Asking for help is an inconvenience to others."
"I have to figure this out on my own."
"If I don't take care of this, no one will."

I know these are not truths, but, whoa, they can really feel like it in my system to this day. I have a hard time delegating tasks or asking for help. Between motherhood and Slumberkins, this grew to be a very heavy load. It broke me down, which I'll share more about later in Chapter 19, "Self-Expression."

This is an example of how so many of us grew up in loving homes with parents who didn't do anything "wrong"; they simply were never taught about emotional wellness themselves. But we are a generation where now that we know the long-term impacts and importance, it's become a necessary skill to understand emotional wellness and development and incorporate it into our own parenting practices. If we don't have the conversations, children will form negative or irrational beliefs that surface in their relationships later in life that they then need to work through. I love that we can be proactive and teach them about these things that will support them for the long term.

A couple of my favorite affirmations to support this part in me that formed from these beliefs in my system are from our Self-Expression (Lynx) and Anxiety (Alpaca) collections when I can feel signs of overwhelm:

I can say what I need. I know I belong. I speak my truth when I feel it. I am worthy and strong.

I am strong and supported. I am never alone. Climbing these mountains will lead me home.

My hope is that my children will have memories of a mother who worked hard but modeled asking for help when she needed to, took breaks before burning out, practiced healthy self-care routines, and opened conversations about feelings around how our family functions along the way.

KELLY'S STORY

From the outside looking in, my life often seems like I have it all together. I have always been good at making sure that I am achieving, being nice, and doing all the "right things."

Growing up, I was praised or rewarded for being pleasant and compliant. I believed that to be "good," I needed to take care of other people.

I just wanted everybody to be happy, and I was willing to ignore my own emotional wants and needs to make that happen.

No one specifically told me that I had to act this way to earn love, but then again, they also never told me I *didn't* need to function this way to earn their love. So, I ended up forming my beliefs based on these experiences, along with this false narrative in my own head.

I ended up forming a core belief that "I am not worthy of love and care, unless I am taking care of my loved one's feelings." So rather than taking care of myself, or even knowing that I was important, I put my focus on taking care of the feelings and needs of others. I always played the same role and had the same outcome—ignoring my own needs, feelings, and desires and instead focusing on someone else's. I felt that I had to abandon myself to make sure everyone else was OK.

As you can imagine, this doesn't work well in an intimate relationship, even though I thought I was being the best partner. What I was giving was based on my own *untrue* core belief from childhood. This belief kept me from being able to tune in to my own emotions in a way that allowed others to be there for me. Ultimately, I have repeated this pattern many times through my relationships in my life and finally (I hope) have gained the awareness and strength to update and change that belief for myself. It's a work in progress, and when I voice my own needs and desires and/or don't center myself around the feelings of others, the inner voice whispers my old fears of abandonment or rejection. It may never go away. However, now I can try to notice and choose myself and my updated positive beliefs in moments that used to take me down a path of self-abandonment.

PERSONALITY TYPES

As core beliefs are formed throughout our lives based on lived experiences, they drive our self-concept and can even drive how our personality is expressed. This is why we extended this knowledge into everything we do at Slumberkins. Each of the characters in the world of Slumberkins has a personality type based on real kids and common personality profiles. You might see yourself in some of these characters, or you might see your child in some of them. We built them with different personalities, strengths, and challenges to help give you tools to support your feelings and deeper core beliefs. No matter who you identify with, you can learn something about yourself or others by getting to know them. Here are a few of the most common personality types represented by some of our Slumberkins characters.

The Perfectionist might be praised for their neat handwriting and out-standing report cards. The praise makes the child feel good and continue to seek perfection. On the other hand, they may be overly critical of themselves or avoid trying new things for fear of falling short of perfection. If this belief continues into adulthood, it can impact their willingness to take risks, and they may not be able to cope well with failure.

In the Slumberkins world, Yak is a challenger and a perfectionist. She is strong and independent and likes to take the lead. She also really likes to work hard to get things to be "just right" and struggles when they are not. She has lots of energy and can be a lot of fun to be around when she is in the flow of things—but she can be challenging when things aren't going how she wants them to go. With a strong sense of justice, Yak is more likely to get into an argument than a lot of her friends because she is willing to fight for what she believes in. That said, she is a kind, thoughtful person, and she is loyal to her good friends.

Strengths: Leadership qualities, speaking up for herself, working hard, trying her best

Struggles: Coping with disappointment and anxiety; letting others take the lead; flexible thinking; making appropriate choices when she is angry; self-acceptance; self-worth when she makes mistakes; impulse control when triggered, if things are not going her way, or when others aren't listening to her

The Caregiver or Helper might be referred to as the "responsible one" in the family, especially in helping care for younger siblings. They might internalize this role to the extent that, as an adult, they feel compelled to always put others' needs before their own, potentially at the cost of their well-being. If a child is frequently praised for being helpful, they might start to believe that their value lies in being useful to others.

Bigfoot is a peacekeeper and a helper. A great friend, he wants others around him to feel good and does his best to help others in need. He's kind and sweet, he has a good sense of humor, and he's easygoing and social. He lifts people up.

Strengths: Friendly, kind, creative, musical, funny, high emotional IQ, adaptable, mature, identifies the strengths of others, empathetic, team player

Struggles: Identifying his own strengths, advocating for himself, setting boundaries with others, self-esteem, shame/embarrassment, people-pleasing, self-consciousness

The Shy One might be naturally quiet in certain social situations. If they start telling themselves that they're "too" quiet, they might start believing that they're inherently unsocial. Avoiding interactions could limit their social development, ultimately affecting their adult confidence in personal and professional relationships.

Sloth is highly imaginative and introverted. Though he can be quite anxious and fearful, he is kind and tends to be a peacemaker. A sweet caretaker who is always thinking about the "little guy," Sloth is quite magical and connected to nature. Because he can be anxious, he benefits from routines and structure and likes to know what is coming next. He is sensitive and thoughtful.

> **Strengths:** Imaginative, creative, thoughtful, stands up for little creatures (the underdog), sensitive
>
> **Struggles:** Coping with anxiety and hurt feelings, standing up for himself, joining groups of kids, knowing what he wants, separation anxiety

The Star may happen to stand out from the crowd on a sports team, or any other persuit that they have committed themselves to. They build their sense of value and worth tied to this persona, whether it's an "athlete" a "star student" or "nerd". It is a pressure and drive to be the star in what they have chosen.

Fox is achievement-focused, ultra-competitive, and independent. An outgoing guy, he loves to have fun and wants to do his best, but he can struggle with anxiety and stress when plans change. Fox often wants to be "tough," and he struggles to show vulnerability and ask for help when needed. Fox can act out at school and home (sometimes aggressively), and he is working on putting words to his feelings and finding healthy outlets for his anger and stress.

Strengths: Fun, strong, outgoing, fast, good at sports, loving, kind, leader
Struggles: Asking for help, adjusting to change, using his words when he is upset, leaning into competition due to low self-esteem

The Clown, who is known for being the class clown and making others laugh, might internalize this role, feeling pressured to always be entertaining and humorous, even in situations where they feel sad or serious. This can lead to them masking their true emotions and struggling with emotional authenticity in their adult life.

Unicorn lives life to the fullest. She is creative, outgoing, and fun, and she looks at things in a special and unique way. She wants everything to have meaning and sometimes gets upset or frustrated when others don't understand her ideas—or aren't as excited as she is about them. She wouldn't typically be described as practical or down-to-earth because she loves living in the world of ideas and creativity.

1. **Strengths:** Creative, fun, playful, kind, marches to the beat of her own drum, inspires creativity in others, high energy, excitable, daydreamer, joker
2. **Struggles:** Explaining ideas to others, coping with adoption, sitting still, coloring inside the lines (metaphorically speaking)

The Smart One, who is often praised for their academic achievements, might start to believe their worth is tied to their intellect. This belief could create undue pressure to always excel academically, leading to stress and anxiety and potentially causing them to shy away from challenges where they might not immediately succeed.

Narwhal is achievement-focused and smart. He is a strong self-critic because he likes to stay ahead of criticism in his own head. Happy and kind-hearted, he is well liked by his peers and teachers because he does well in school.

    Strengths: Motivated, high-achieving in school, competitive, team player, natural leader
    Struggles: Handling critiques, acting defensive, accepting support from others, focusing on activities without a clear goal

Though some of these personality types might feel extremely similar to you or someone you know, remember that we have the capacity to be more than "just one thing." We want to arm our children with the knowledge that they can get their needs met even if they stray from the "type" of person they consider themselves to be. If kids start to believe that they are "stuck" being one type of person, they will miss opportunities for emotional growth and development.

WHY CORE BELIEFS ARE SO IMPORTANT

Core beliefs affect the way we feel about ourselves; they impact our relationships, our emotions, and our decisions. They are the beliefs about ourselves that shape our reality, guiding our thoughts, behaviors, and emotional responses. Think about how your life, your choices, and your feelings about yourself may change if you believe something like "I am unlovable" versus "I am lovable."

CORE BELIEFS IN ACTION

Have you ever wondered why two people can experience the same thing but have very different reactions? What is "really" happening in any given situation gets filtered through our core beliefs lens. Later, we create a story about the experience. If we have different core beliefs than someone else, we may have a totally different perspective or story about what happened.

For example, a family in the neighborhood is having a birthday party and two children haven't been invited. Child A has the core belief "I will never belong." When they hear about the party, they may think, "Of course they didn't invite me. I knew they didn't really like me anyway. When it comes time for my birthday party, I'm not going to invite them!"

Child B, who was also not invited, may have a different interpretation of the situation. If they have the core beliefs "I am lovable" and "I belong," they may think, "I wish I'd been invited. Maybe if I invite them to my birthday party, we can get to know each other better. I'll invite a good friend over today because I always feel better after we play."

Both children may feel similar emotions—like sadness or loneliness—but their core beliefs create very different stories about what happened. Adaptive core beliefs don't necessarily shift our feelings (the kids can be sad or disappointed or mad about not being invited because feelings are always OK just as they are), but they do shift how we interpret events—and even what actions we take afterward.

While we can't always change what is happening around us, we can tune in to our core beliefs and shift the narrative we tell ourselves. Doing so not only feels better but also increases our inherent kindness, confidence, and resiliency. The really good news is that we can help our kids tune in to—and name—their core beliefs and also shift any negative beliefs into more adaptive beliefs.

Children have a limited, often black-or-white, understanding of the world around them. So when they undergo difficult experiences that leave them feeling conflicted, confused, or upset, negative core beliefs may form. Although these negative beliefs are often untrue or inaccurate, they can *feel* true and accurate. Because they were formed with the more limited perspective and self-centered view of a child, they continue to be limited, even if those beliefs persist through adulthood.

When children go through tough times, they tell themselves stories to make sense of the situation, often blaming themselves even when the fault doesn't lie with them. These stories, which may or may not be true, help children protect themselves when the reality of the situation is too much to process. Making up a story about it helps them work through the moment and keeps them feeling connected to their caregivers.

In the previous example, someone who believes "I am unlovable" and doesn't get invited to a birthday party might make up a story about why they were overlooked; they might decide that they were too loud or too pushy or too clingy and take those assumptions into future relationships. Many of us likely don't realize that we carry around deep negative core beliefs. We believe them even if we don't know if they're true or not. Experts understand that our deeply held beliefs impact our behavior, thoughts, feelings, and relationships more than our logically held beliefs.

SAMPLE CORE BELIEFS

This is a list of common core beliefs that are often formed in early childhood. Remember, core beliefs can always be changed and adapted through connection and learning.

NEGATIVE BELIEF	POSITIVE BELIEF
I am alone	I am always connected to those I love
I am not important	I am important
I am invisible	I can find people to "see" me
I am powerless	I have inner strength
I have to be in control	I can recognize what I can and cannot control
I should have done something more	I did what I could
I am unlovable	I am lovable
I am defective/worthless	I am wonderful just the way that I am
I am in danger	I am protected/I can seek help when I need it
I am not good enough	I am good enough just the way I am

As a therapist, I worked with adults who were struggling with negative core beliefs. These beliefs were blocking them from being able to be at their best in their relationships, work, and lives. Like many therapists across the globe, I was helping them identify and adjust these beliefs by creating healing moments for them. The goal was to adjust those beliefs to be more in line with their current experience. Francine Shapiro, PhD (EMDR), identified core belief clusters that most of these beliefs will fall into. They are safety/vulnerability, control/choice, worthiness/lovability, guilt/shame, and responsibility/survival. (We'll take a closer look at these in Chapter 4, "Connect-to-Grow: Breaking Down the Approach.") We took some of these tools and ideas and integrated them into Slumberkins to help parents do this work for themselves while helping their children form positive core beliefs from the beginning.

—Kelly

CORE BELIEF STAGES

You can find the core beliefs that are formed during the first four stages of emotional development in Chapter 2, "Stages of Emotional Development," but we'll list them again here to give you some additional context. You can see a through line between these beliefs and the developmental stages of emotional learning. As you're reading, also consider the potential impact that experiences and environments in the early years of childhood have on your child's core beliefs.

Stage 1: Babies (0 to 18 Months)

- "I am safe."
- "I am valued."
- "My needs are important."

Children in the infant stages are so dependent on their caregivers that negative experiences in this developmental stage can make them prone to negative core beliefs relating to safety and support. Babies learn quickly what to expect from the people and world around them and form neural pathways in their brains to solidify this learning. The brain is developing such foundational knowledge at this point that these beliefs and felt experiences can stay with people for a long time (we can also heal later, though!).

Stage 2: Toddlers (18 Months to 3 Years)

- "I am capable."
- "I can do things myself."
- "It's OK to be independent."

As children test their autonomy, they explore different aspects of their personalities and test the types of responses they get. They are in an egocentric state of development, so they often fall into traps of attributing situations to themselves (like divorce, family conflict, and so on), leading to core beliefs that they are "bad" or things are "their fault." Because of their often strong emotional reactions, little kids can sometimes elicit strong feelings from adults, which can lead to feelings of shame or worry about not being loved or welcome. Core beliefs about control and choice might form during this stage.

Stage 3: Little Kid (3 Years to 5 Years)

- "I can make good things happen."
- "My ideas are valuable."

Here, children realize the value of their contribution to others as they work to "master" skills. They want to run fast, climb high, read, write, learn math, draw . . . you name it, they are working at it. Sometimes this can lead to associating their abilities or skills with their worth (some of us adults do this, too). If their contributions seem welcome and useful, positive beliefs form. If not, they may begin to doubt themselves and their abilities.

Stage 4: Big Kid (5 Years to 13 Years)

- "I am competent."
- "I can succeed."

In this stage, kids are ready to dive deeper into the skills and preferences they felt drawn to in their learning from the previous stage. Reminding kids that they are enough even when they make mistakes and that they are lovable just the way they are is essential during this time. This makes it clear that the competence and preferences that they are exploring are aligned with interest and desire, rather than coming from a place of "need" for acceptance and love. When we support our children in fostering self-esteem and proactively set them up with stability and support, they will be more prepared to navigate those intense times to come.

Though core beliefs can form at any age, children are especially susceptible to negative beliefs at certain times during their emotional development, which is why we should be as vigilant as possible to make sure our children are forming positive core beliefs.

Traumatic experiences that are a struggle for us to process can also affect the stories we tell ourselves, whether we're children or adults. When a traumatic event occurs, our brains are wired to lean toward negative beliefs. But the good news is that we can heal ourselves and shift these beliefs.

Sometimes the things we say to kids or model through our own behaviors get passed on to our little ones. That's why doing the work on our own core beliefs is so important. We've gotten lots of feedback from adults that our books and affirmations help *them* just as much as they help their children!

—Kelly

USING CORE BELIEFS TO FIND OUR INNER VOICE

You know that voice you hear in your head all day long? The one that guides your thoughts, feelings, holds internal debates, and can be your cheerleader or your worst critic? Meet your inner voice.

Children are not born with an inner voice. A child's inner voice does not come online until around the age of 7. Seven. And up until then, it's being formed by everything around them as they make sense of the world and try to make meaning out of their experiences. These are the years you can make the biggest impact, so it's especially important to focus on helping your child form their inner voice during these years. A child consistently met with warmth and encouragement is likely to develop a positive inner voice, while one who faces criticism or neglect may develop a more negative self-dialogue. This is why this window is so crucial to guide our children on their path to building positive core beliefs about themselves.

Understanding core beliefs is like uncovering the roots of a tree, providing nourishment and direction for the branches that reach outward. The inner voice, a crucial aspect of our mental landscape, is significantly shaped by these core beliefs. It's like a tape that plays in our heads, often echoing what we've heard and internalized from our early caregivers and significant life experiences. This voice can be nurturing, encouraging us with affirmations, or it can be critical, reinforcing doubts and fears.

In the early stages of development, the inner voice is not a personal experience but a shared one between child and caregivers. The things we say to our little ones and the behaviors we model become their inner voice. Once their inner voice is established (roughly by age 7), what a child says in their head—and out loud—becomes their identity. They are the creator of their story, and what they say, what they choose to focus on, becomes their reality.

HOW TO IDENTIFY YOUR OWN CORE BELIEFS

Sometimes the best way to help your child is to look inward at your own deeply held beliefs. Taking a few moments to reflect on how you move through the world will help you become more aware of how you are modeling behavior and self-talk for your child. Doing so will help your child learn to move through the world, too. It does take some introspection and self-awareness to identify your own core beliefs, so here are some steps to guide you through this process:

1. **Look at the personality types described earlier:** Do you resonate with one or more of these common personality types? Sometimes we can't quite grasp our core beliefs, but we can tell they are there by our emotional reactions. Start by reflecting on your emotional responses to experiences that felt charged to you—consider a time when you felt trapped by your "personality type." Ask yourself what these reactions reveal about your beliefs.

2. **Examine your self-talk:** Pay attention to the narrative that runs in your mind, especially during challenging times. Negative self-talk often reflects underlying core beliefs. Phrases like "I always mess things up" or "I can't do anything right" can indicate beliefs about incompetence or unworthiness.

3. **Analyze patterns in your relationships:** Do you tend to stay in unfulfilling relationships because you believe you don't deserve better? Do you avoid getting close to others because you believe they'll eventually hurt you? Search for commonalities in the way you relate to others.

4. **Consider your upbringing:** Reflect on messages you received during childhood. Parents, teachers, and early experiences significantly shape our core beliefs. Think about the expectations and values that were emphasized in your family and how they might have influenced your self-perception.

5. **Identify your fears:** Fears often point to core beliefs. If you fear failure, you might believe that your worth is tied to success. If you fear rejection, you might believe that you're not inherently lovable or acceptable.

6. **Journal:** Writing about your experiences and feelings can help uncover patterns that indicate core beliefs. Look for themes in your entries over time.

7. **Seek feedback:** Sometimes, it's hard to see our own patterns. Trusted friends, family members, or a therapist can offer insights into beliefs you might be holding unconsciously.

   We love therapy! A therapist or counselor can be immensely helpful in guiding you to identify and understand your core beliefs, especially those deeply embedded and hard to recognize.

This journey of self-discovery may feel uncomfortable or intimidating, but if you stick with it, it can lead to significant personal growth and transformation. By understanding—and occasionally reevaluating—your core beliefs, you open the door to a more authentic and fulfilling life, and you are better equipped to lead your child through their own path of discovery.

Remember that while some core beliefs can be empowering, others might hold you back. Make sure you spend time discerning whether certain core beliefs serve your well-being or need to be reassessed. Striving for this degree of self-awareness allows you to become more in line with your true values and helps you to become a positive role model for your child.

CHAPTER 4

Connect-to-Grow: Breaking Down the Approach

You've learned the background on your child's emotional development, you understand the importance of core beliefs, you've learned how the inner voice is formed . . . and now you're ready for the Connect-to-Grow approach. Our method will show you how to lean in and embrace the responsibility of being your child's first teacher of emotional health. It's uncomplicated, it's easy to implement, and it's doable for anyone, no matter where they are on their own emotional growth journey.

It has always been our mission to help solve a problem by helping children help themselves. Teachers are happy when their students move up a grade. Therapists are happy when their clients may not need sessions any longer. Moving on ideally means that learning has taken place and that children are out there in the world utilizing their new skills in a way that is beneficial to themselves and to others.

In the same way, we hope that we will give you skills and strategies to continue helping your children grow, both now and in the future. Our primary focus will be to give you what you want—information to help you better connect with your child. We also want you to know that it's equally important for you to connect with yourself. In fact, your connection to yourself will have the biggest impact on your ability and capacity to connect with your child. Never forget that you and your emotional health matter when it comes to your child's emotional development.

We know the responsibility of raising a good human can be daunting in our state of overwhelm and burnout as parents. Think of the Connect-to-Grow approach as your daily emotional fitness routine with your kids. It's simple on purpose because we believe that positive skill building and emotional wellness happen when you are consistent, and it's easier to be consistent when the process is manageable. Let's break it down together.

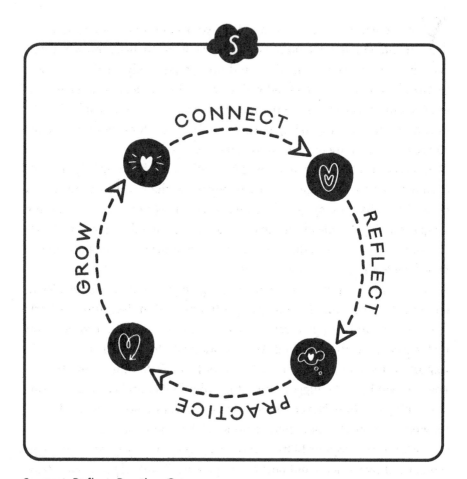

Connect. Reflect. Practice. Grow.

By implementing this approach into your family life, your kids will feel more connected, seen, loved, and supported. They'll have the skills to create, maintain, and navigate relationships and the inevitable difficulties that come with life. Proactively building this emotional foundation will ideally inoculate your child to some of the trials and tribulations that may arise as they grow.

Connect   Reflect   Practice   Grow

These icons appear in each chapter to indicate which part of the Connect-to-Grow approach the strategy being discussed addresses.

CONNECT

From our perspective, connection is everything. That's why connection is the first step of this approach. In its simplest form, "connect" refers to the way we interact with ourselves and our children. Connection means having an experience of emotional resonance, either with yourself or with someone else, and it's through this connection that all learning starts. It's how we make meaning and have purpose in our lives. It's through our connections to ourselves and each other that we discover our reason for being, thus driving our emotional capacity and fulfillment throughout life. Parents are the best teachers of your child's emotional health and wellness, and we want to equip you for the journey.

Connection to Self for Parents

Before we can connect with others, we must first connect with ourselves. Connection to Self is essential because our understanding of ourselves defines the way we move through the world and approach our lives. Remember the self-work and awareness we just did around our own core beliefs in Chapter 3? Connection to Self is the reason it's so important to understand ourselves and our reactions to overwhelm, stress, or discomfort. Being able to connect with yourself, check in, self-regulate, and take a breath become some of the most important skills in your parent arsenal.

Connection to Self in practice for adults can be simply carving out time to tune in to yourself. It can be going for a walk, meditating, or giving yourself those extra five minutes in the driveway to sit in silence before stepping into the house and being bombarded with requests. It's about meeting your own needs first. Depending on where we are on our own emotional wellness journey, connecting to your Self can look different for everyone. Connection to Self can overlap with self-care, which we know not many of us busy parents have time for, but like any other practice, it actually gets easier as you continue to learn how to tune in, assess your own emotional state, and come up with a plan (if needed) to help you self-regulate. But again, this takes practice.

For example, Kelly prefers meditation and mindfulness practices. For Kelly, connection to Self looks like a 10- to 20-minute guided meditation that helps her reset and stay grounded. Callie prefers to be physically active, get outside, and take a walk. It's a true mind-body connection and helps regulate the emotions that she may need to process.

The benefit of being connected to Self as a parent is the ability to be present with your child. Because you're in alignment with your own needs, you have space to tune in to your child's needs, helping you return to the sense of wonder, curiosity, and joy that you unconsciously possessed as a child. Kids arrive in the world wired with a glass-half-full attitude, and all the work that parents do is to try to get back to that place. Connecting to Self helps us return to that attitude we possessed as children, except now we are proceeding in a more conscious way. You can understand your own Self through seeing your child and recognizing that they—and you—are a fully embodied, worthy, beautiful human.

We know it can be hard to start this practice as a parent when you're functioning in overwhelm. You might feel like you're just hanging on and counting the minutes until bedtime. We've been there, so we are keeping you in mind as we explore what Connect-to-Grow looks like in practice. In Part 2, "Putting It into Practice," we'll be leading you through "connect to Self" reflection moments around each topic or situation to guide you into alignment with your sense of childhood wonder. Think about them as your oxygen mask moments. We've got you.

Connection to Self for parents might look like:

- Slowing down and becoming aware of your thoughts
- Physical activity—what is your body needing? (rest, movement, stretching)
- Meditation
- Journaling
- Doing any activity that makes you feel like you're "in the zone"

Connection to Self for Kids

Instinctually, kids experience everything in a very present state (which is easier to do when you don't have an inner voice yet!). They form an understanding of Self by seeing themselves through their caregiver's eyes. The more we can help them understand their own power and be a reflection of their true and most authentic selves, the better off they're going to be.

It will be through the process of engaging in reflection with you that your child will start to build up their self-concept. Remember, the formation of the inner voice occurs during this time, and we are continually guiding them through that process. This is a continuous journey. It evolves as children grow, with each stage presenting new opportunities for emotional development. Your empathy, patience, and guidance are the cornerstones of this journey, helping your child build a foundation of self-awareness and emotional resilience.

In the end, the goal is to empower your child with a strong sense of Self so that they feel loved, understood, and capable of navigating their emotional world. This journey, filled with its unique challenges and joys, is one of the most rewarding aspects of parenting. By nurturing this connection to Self from infancy through the toddler years and beyond, you're not only supporting your child's emotional growth but also laying the groundwork for a confident, self-assured individual.

Connection Between Parent and Child

The importance of connection between parent and child is the reason we started Slumberkins in the first place; it is the basis of everything we do. We often say:

> *The emotional health and wellness of your child is not separate from your own as the parent.*

If you really think about that, it makes self-care and connection to Self even more important. After all, you can't pour from an empty cup, so you need to make sure your cup is full before being able to support your child. We truly believe that for us to show up and take good care of others—our kids—we must first take good care of ourselves. Your own emotional wellness is *as important* as your child's.

Taking the extra time to connect with your child when you have had a long day at work and have a to-do list a mile long can be exhausting, but it's essential. It's why we published a line of books that gives parents the script to show up and connect in a focused and meaningful way, even in moments of overwhelm. That way, even if you're feeling exhausted and uncreative, all you have to do to forge a connection is read the words on the page. You don't need to have a Slumberkins book, though. Connection between parents and kids means simply showing up and giving your child the gift of presence. Even in small increments, presence is ultimately the most powerful piece of the puzzle of parenting in today's world of overwhelm, technology, and disconnection.

The Slumberkins books will facilitate moments of connection in the simplest possible way—you just

have to read the book out loud with your child. Each book is written by a family therapist with words that empower you to take the lead in supporting the development of a specific emotional skill with your child.

But whether you use Slumberkins or not, we will help you find these meaningful moments throughout the day. Our ready-to-use books and content simply make the process easy to implement; you can just grab a book and know that you're doing and saying exactly what your child needs to hear.

As we watch our own kids grow, we now have the opportunity to take a look at how we were raised and "programmed" by our parents, experiences, and environment. We can assess what we want to repeat or what we want to improve upon for our own child's experience. We can investigate the programming we received in childhood and evaluate the things we learned are true and necessary and helpful. We can decide which values, viewpoints, parenting strategies, and outdated thoughts might not serve the next generation. We can decide which learnings we want to share with our children and which may be an outdated way of thinking that will not serve the next generation.

The connection between parent and child runs deep and will continue to deepen over time, especially after your child becomes a parent themselves.

Connection between parent and child might look like:

- Giving your child your undivided attention
- Joining their world through play
- Sharing stories—kids are interested to know about how you were when you were little
- Sharing your family history or values and beliefs
- Cuddling or playing together (physical play)

Repair: Returning to Connection

In every relationship, moments of disconnection or misunderstanding are inevitable. Humans simply aren't designed to stay in a state of connection 24/7, and sometimes (actually quite often), we flat-out screw it up. We will inevitably lose our temper and scream at our kids even when they're not necessarily what's upsetting us. We may actually be upset about something we haven't addressed with our partner, our tech devices are driving us to distraction, or we're stressed about a presentation at work. Or maybe we overreacted to a normal kid issue, like a sibling conflict or a morning meltdown.

"If they would just behave, I wouldn't have had to yell!" Have you ever had that thought? What's really happening is you're allowing your own big feelings to take over and putting the weight of your emotional regulation in your child's hands. Instead, think about the way you want your kids to handle themselves when their big feelings take over. You'd want them to take a deep breath, take a break if they need to, use their words to communicate, apologize, and take accountability. Our kids are observing us in these moments, and the way we react teaches them how to react. Because conflicts, overwhelm, and disconnection are guaranteed as they grow through their lives, modeling repair sets them up for relational success.

REPAIR IN ACTION

How can we repair after moments of disconnection?

1. Acknowledge the issue or disconnection.
2. Take accountability for *your* part (even if it came after theirs).
3. Talk about the need behind your feelings.
4. Discuss how *you* will work to do it different next time.
5. Apologize and reconnect (don't rush to the next step).
6. Ask their perspective and support them in trying to do steps 1–5 if they feel ready.

Check in: Don't force a fake apology from your child. Sometimes we may have to take the lead a few times through this process and model a sincere apology ourselves before real apologies start coming from our kids, especially if we have not been repairing in this way before.

Ask them these questions:

1. What do you think happened?
2. What did you feel when that happened?
3. What did you need or want to happen instead?
4. Empathize with feeling/need (maybe even tell a story when you have felt that way).
5. Can we think of another way to (insert need/feeling here) take care of that?
6. I said sorry to you. Did that help you know that I want to do it differently next time?

Check in: Don't use your feelings to get them to apologize. Your feelings are not their responsibility—they are yours.

> You can say, "It makes me feel good to know that we are going to try something different and you don't want to [scream and hit me or other problem]. It helps us move forward together when we both know that we are going to try to do better. We are both learning, and we love each other no matter what."
>
> You might also say, "I told you that I was sorry. Did that help you know that I want to do it differently next time? Because it would help me to know that you're sorry and want to do things differently next time, too."

For so many of our parents and their parents before them, apologizing to a child was not the norm. They came from a time when "children are meant to be seen, not heard" or were expected to respect and obey their parents, no matter how their parents were treating them. We know now that it is through our early relationships that we learn *how* to repair, apologize, and connect with our loved ones. We want those relationships to be based on respect and care, but if we want our kids to embody these qualities, so must we.

If we have never experienced our own parents apologizing to us or modeling this to us, we often feel entitled to continue that pattern with our own children, thereby passing down a pattern of disconnection and difficulty with repair.

Repair is how we build strength in our relationships and how we build trust and take accountability when we make mistakes. When it comes to our kids, it is important to remember we must be the role models for them. Of course they did something to warrant a reaction from you, but if that reaction was harsh, scared them, or was not coming from a balanced place in you, then it's time to practice what you preach and show your child how to take accountability, apologize, communicate your needs, and repair.

It's a hard skill, especially when you are leading the charge as an adult who never received this from your own parents. But it gets easier with time, and your kids will be learning this skill early, which will definitely be helpful to your relationship as they enter the pre-teen and teenage years to come.

Repair can be as simple as apologizing for a misunderstanding, actively listening to your child's perspective, or spending quality time together to re-establish the bond. The act of repair goes beyond mere conflict resolution; it's about reaffirming trust and reinforcing the understanding that the love and bond you share with your child are unconditional and enduring.

The importance of repair in our connections is as crucial as forging those connections in the first place. Though the need to use repair may seem like you did something "wrong," these instances, though challenging, offer valuable opportunities for growth and deepening bonds. The process of coming back into connection after a conflict or a period of disconnection underscores the resilience and strength of your relationship with your child. It teaches them that while misunderstandings and mistakes are part of life, they do not define the entirety of a relationship. This process instills in children the confidence that they are valued and heard, even in times of conflict, fostering a secure attachment that is vital for their emotional development.

REFLECT

When you inevitably experience moments of disconnection with your child, engaging in reflection is key. Take time to reflect on what was happening for you or your child, notice what concerns arise, and think about the hope you have for your future interactions. It's in the moments of reflection that we hone our awareness and integrate learning that comes from that awareness. That way, we return to our connection with a new perspective or awareness that we can put into practice.

In this approach, reflection can have two different meanings: reflecting your child's feelings, responses, and actions back to them, *and* slowing down and engaging in the process of self-reflection.

Mirroring and Reflecting: Supporting Your Child's Feelings, Responses, and Actions

We can help children establish their connection to Self starting from infancy. From the earliest moments, children experience the world with a present, instinctual curiosity. Their understanding of Self is profoundly shaped by how they perceive themselves through your eyes. As parents, our role in mirroring their true and authentic selves, understanding their emotional landscape, and aiding in their self-discovery is invaluable.

In infancy, a critical way to foster this connection to Self is through the practice of "mirroring" your child and attentively meeting their physical needs. Mirroring involves reflecting the emotions or facial expressions your child displays. When your child smiles and you smile back or when they express sadness and you respond with a similar expression, it's more than mere imitation. This is a vital form of emotional attunement that helps your child feel seen, understood, and connected. This simple yet profound interaction assures them of your love and care. It lays the foundation of trust and security, crucial for their ongoing emotional development and self-connection.

As your child steps into the toddler years, the focus shifts to integrating routines and fostering independence. You can support them in identifying basic emotions and learning coping strategies. Remember, your role isn't to fix their feelings but to guide them in recognizing, accepting, and expressing these emotions. Encouraging independence, whether it's in small tasks like choosing their clothes or helping with simple chores, bolsters their confidence and self-esteem. This phase, which is pivotal for reinforcing their connection to Self, is about nurturing their emerging sense of autonomy while providing the secure base from which they can explore the world.

As they move into the preschool and school years, your child's experiences are more than just physical milestones; they are stepping stones in their emotional maturation. Supporting them in naming their feelings, understanding the cause and effect of their actions, and acknowledging their right to their emotions cultivate a robust sense of Self. It's through these everyday interactions, the acknowledgment of their efforts, and your consistent emotional availability that your child learns the value of their inner voice and feelings.

What Does Reflection Look Like for Little and Big Kids?

Reflecting an infant's feelings or helping a toddler name their emotions is fairly straightforward. Reflecting for your preschool or elementary-school child might feel like more of a challenge. Let's run through some everyday scenarios in which reflection might come into play.

If your child happens to be sad because you're having tacos instead of pizza for dinner, you may be tempted to say something along the lines of "Here's something that will make you feel better." Or if it's been a long day you might resort to "If you're going to cry, go cry in your room." After all, the majority of us have been programmed to either fix or shut down any show of big emotions.

Instead, you can be an observer of body language, saying, "Your eyes are watering. You're holding your breath. You're looking at your feet. Are you . . . sad?" Even if it seems clear to you which emotion your child is feeling, ask the question. The answer might not always be what you think it is. When you ask, you give your child the chance to agree or substitute a different emotion.

A great phrase to have in your parent toolkit is "I'm curious." As in, "You look like you might cry. I'm curious . . . are you feeling sad?" Or, "I'm curious . . . you seem sad right now. Is that what you're feeling?" The word *curious* demonstrates that you have a genuine interest in how your child is feeling. You're not looking to sweep things under the rug and move on. You are showing that you truly want to know what's going on. Curiosity (or asking others about their perspective) is such a powerful tool. All people want to feel seen and understood, including children. If we can help fill in the blanks with words and support them in labeling their internal experiences, they begin to learn how to do this on their own—leading to great self-awareness.

Most kids, especially young kids, are going to go for the more black-and-white response of "Yes, I'm sad" or "I'm mad." Or maybe they'll just shrug. If they don't answer or say they don't know how they're feeling, you can say, "It looks like you might be sad. If you're sad, we should talk about it." Be open to any (or no) response. Leaving room for more acknowledgment, connection, and understanding breeds the space for vulnerability, which is a key ingredient to connection and belonging and all of the essentials that you want in a parent-child relationship.

The key to it all is that feeling of belonging, safety, feeling seen, feeling loved—that no matter what emotion is coming up, your child always knows they're going to be OK.

Reflection Tips

- Give your child your full attention.
- Look them in the eye.
- Prioritize understanding over responding.
- Don't be afraid of silence.
- Name and describe or narrate emotions.
- Take a guess at what they are feeling; don't be afraid to let them correct you.

Self-Reflection and Modeling

When children feel seen, heard, and understood by their parents, they build an internal foundation that can include the practice of self-reflection. Self-reflection is the learning that we all want our kids to have access to. For example, after a fight with a sibling, we want our kids to learn from the interaction and thoughtfully approach things differently next time. We can help them in this process by asking questions about the *why* behind their behavior, their feelings, and their needs. This process actually takes a lot of regulation and brain power, so adults need to support and model this process in the early years. This way children not only learn the skills but also see those skills put into action through their connection with adults.

Self-reflection is a way to notice, consider, and learn from experiences. We're trying to teach our children to ask themselves: What am I feeling? What is going on with me? Why did I make that decision? Was my reaction too big or small? Did I react or respond?

To encourage self-reflection in your child, you can actively share examples like these with them:

WHAT TO DO	WHAT THIS SOUNDS LIKE
Say things out loud that you hope your child will start saying to themselves	"I'm going to try to color inside the lines today, but if I don't, I'm not worried! I'll still make a great picture."
Approach difficult feelings with curiosity rather than judgment	"My body feels so tense and angry today, and I can't figure out why."
Use deep breathing or body regulation techniques	"It seems like we're both frustrated. Let's take a deep breath together and figure out what to do next."
Review decisions and events once everyone is in a calm state	"Wow, it seemed like you were really angry when you slammed the door a few minutes ago. What was going on? Is there anything else you can do when you're angry?"

Some children pick up on this technique quickly, and others take a longer time to understand. Keep staying the course. The first time your child transitions from a wordless screaming tantrum into saying "I AM SO ANGRY RIGHT NOW!" you'll know that this work is making an impact.

Try Modeling Your Own Feelings

As educators, we learned a process called *metacognition*, in which you share your awareness and understanding of your own thought processes out loud with your class, modeling what a learner's thought process might be around a given lesson or objective. It's equally powerful to do this at home for your kids when it comes to awareness and managing your own emotions.

When you talk about what you're feeling before talking about what your child is feeling, it can help them understand and identify feelings as they are seeing them in real time. We all know how fast emotional situations can escalate, and by slowing down and narrating our own feelings and emotional choices, we bring learning and insight into everyday moments that our children can learn from.

While your child is starting to have a meltdown, you might say, "I'm noticing that it's so loud in here that my shoulders are getting tight. My body is telling me I'm getting overwhelmed. I need to have more quiet. Do you think we can make this room a quieter space, or should I take a break? I need to do some deep breathing to calm down."

You can follow up (either in that moment or later when everyone is calm) by asking "Do you ever feel like that?" Asking for your child's perspective puts them in the driver's seat and makes them feel like an expert, like you're in a reciprocal relationship. Step out of the mindset that you're the parent and you know everything; let your child know that you're on this emotional learning journey together. You're showing them that it's OK to take feedback, check in with your emotions, and ultimately be the caretaker of your feelings. The more your child is engaged in identifying, learning, and applying these skills, whether it be to help themselves or you, the better it is for everyone.

It's pretty common to get defensive when someone tells us how we are feeling if we aren't fully aware, especially if the implication is that we shouldn't be feeling that way. For example, imagine that you're fighting with your partner and your voice is raised. They ask, "Why are you so angry right now?" and you say (still yelling), "I'm not angry!" Or maybe you've been told to "calm down" when you're at the height of an emotional breakdown and all you're really trying to do is get your point across, be heard, and be understood. What we need in that moment is for someone to see the *need* behind the behavior.

Our kids are the angry person in this situation all the time. Behind every one of their behaviors, they have a need. While our children's needs may feel trivial to us as adults, they are essential to them. Suggesting to them that their needs aren't important feels exactly like that time you were shut down by your partner.

In essence, this approach and process of connecting and reflecting sets you up to create an emotionally safe container in your relationship so that both sides know that their feelings are welcome, valid, and important. In this dynamic with your child, your job as a parent is to not try to change or fix any feeling but to find the need or message that's behind it. Doing so creates emotional safety for your child.

Key takeaways:

- Reflection means reflecting your child's feelings, responses, and actions back to them
- Reflection can also mean slowing down and engaging in the process of self-reflection
- Approach your child's feelings with sincere curiosity
- Be prepared to accept any response (or no response)
- Remind yourself that behind every behavior is a need

PRACTICE

We include practice as part of the Connect-to-Grow approach because we will constantly be coming in and out of connection, making mistakes, and learning as we grow. In essence, we never stop practicing (and learning as we do so). Practice isn't always easy, especially if your nerves are frayed because you have a Stage-Five Clinger who follows you around the house saying "Mom? Mom? Mom? Mommmmmyyyyyy?" all day.

But it is a balance, and creating that emotionally safe space is the foundation for relationships with more emotional safety being cultivated throughout our kids' lives.

We won't always get it right, we will definitely blow up, mess up, get annoyed, and be overwhelmed by our beautiful and wonderful children. But we keep showing up for them again and again. Think about it like emotional fitness: consistency over time and being diligent in the process of modeling reflection will yield your long-term goal of improving emotional wellness for your family.

Kids will start to generalize the learning and skills we teach them and test them in different situations. Affirmations can help a great deal with practice. Affirmations—or positive, impactful statements about ourselves—are little takeaways that can remind us of the experiences we want to have. They're a kind of shortcut or reminder to help you and your children plug into the feeling of connection. They can help you continue to reinforce emotional skills you want to instill in your child.

How Affirmations Support Core Beliefs and the Inner Voice

Since our core beliefs significantly influence how we perceive the world and ourselves, affirmations become an extremely helpful tool. By using affirmations, children can develop a more positive and empowering perception of themselves and their capabilities, which can influence their actions and decisions. Affirmations help take external praise like "You did a good job" and internalize it into "I did a good job." They allow a child to start saying positive statements about themselves, creating a strong, supportive inner voice.

Affirmations can also instill a sense of resilience in children. When faced with challenges, children who practice affirmations may be more likely to have a positive mindset; they can draw upon their positive core beliefs to persevere and overcome difficulties. When children consistently hear and say positive statements about themselves, they start to internalize these beliefs. This positivity can counteract negative thoughts and beliefs.

You don't need to have a specific problem or be going through a rough patch to use positive affirmations, however. A daily affirmation practice can help kids build positive thinking patterns and core beliefs at any time. But when a situation does arise, having practiced those affirmations can help kids face challenges head-on.

An example of seeing this in action with my own kids has been during sibling conflicts between my daughter and son, who are 18 months apart in age. When they get into a fight and ultimately need to apologize to each other, they can sometimes default to the unempathetic "Soooorrrrrrry" while they look the other way and throw in an eyeroll or two.

I step in and remind them that they actually already know what they need to do. I'll say, "Hold on, remember we've practiced this with Hammerhead."

Then, sometimes with support and sometimes independently, they say this affirmation from *Hammerhead's Recess Challenge*:

- "I felt mad, now I'm calm."
- "I can use my words instead."
- "I'm sorry I hurt you."
- "I still want to be friends."

We've read this affirmation together over and over in times of connection. So every time we practice saying an affirmation in a real-life moment, it helps solidify the learning we've already done. It de-escalates the conflict, initiates repair, reminds them of that place of connection, and allows them the opportunity to practice their emotional skills.

—Callie

*This affirmation is specific to the *Hammerhead's Recess Challenge* book in our Slumberkins collection.

You, as well as your child, can use the positive language in affirmations to:

- Motivate yourself to do something challenging
- Help you cope with challenges and changes
- Boost your self-esteem, mood, and attitude
- Combat negative beliefs about yourself or your abilities
- Help bring about positive changes in your life

Affirmations That You Can Start Using Today

Affirmations don't have to be complicated. In fact, sometimes, the most helpful affirmations are quite simple and easy to remember. When teaching them to children, affirmations should be something they can easily understand and apply. Here are some examples:

- "I am smart."
- "I am focused."
- "I am brave."
- "I am strong."

Different affirmations might work better for different children. A child who needs some support with self-esteem might benefit from the powerful affirmation "The world is better because I am here." Or, a kid who needs a little boost when dealing with a new environment or situation could use a daily affirmation of "I can try new things."

In each of the chapters in Part 2, we'll give you affirmations to practice that help to proactively build the emotional skills or be a support for when you need them.

Here are some examples of common core brief clusters and the affirmations that can be used to support them:

ACHIEVEMENT

PERFECTIONISM

I must never fail or make a mistake.

PERCEIVED PERFECTIONISM

People will not love and accept me as a flawed and vulnerable human being.

I don't have to be perfect,
I can just be.
I am loved and enough,
by just being me.

LOVE

APPROVAL ADDICTION

I need everyone's approval to be worthwhile.

FEAR OF REJECTION

If you reject me, it proves something is wrong with me. If I'm alone, I'm bound to feel miserable and worthless.

I am true to myself.
I let my light shine.
I can be who I am.
That's for me to define.

SUBMISSIVENESS

PLEASING OTHERS

I should always try to please
others, even if I make myself
miserable and worthless.

SELF-BLAME

The problems in my relationships
are bound to be my fault.

I can say what I need.
I know I belong.
I speak my truth when I feel it.
I am worthy and strong.

DEMANDINGNESS

OTHER-BLAME

The problems in my relationships
are the other person's fault.

ENTITLEMENT

You should always treat me
in the way I expect.

I can be mad,
and let my feelings show.
I will always be loved,
in my heart I know.

DEPRESSION CLUSTER

HOPELESSNESS

My problems could never be solved.
I could never feel truly happy or fulfilled.

WORTHLESSNESS/INFERIORITY

I'm worthless, defective,
and inferior to others.

I can do hard things,
and get through tough days.
I am strong and supported
in so many ways.

ANXIETY CLUSTER

EMOTIONAL PERFECTIONISM

I should always feel happy,
confident, and in control.

PERCEIVED NARCISSISM

The people I care about are demanding,
manipulative, and powerful.

I feel very deeply.
It's a powerful gift.
There is a strength inside me.
To guide and uplift.

OTHER

LOW FRUSTRATION TOLERANCE

I should never be frustrated.
Life should be easy.

SUPERHUMAN

I should always be strong
and never be weak.

I can do hard things.
I can pause or push through.
I trust my body and heart.
I know what to do.

The practice of saying affirmations out loud is a way to build your child's sense of Self so that when it's challenged out there in the world, they can remember the positive input you've given them. The impact affirmations can have in moments of loneliness, anxiety, or depression later in life is profound.

> Words spoken out loud have power. It's why affirmations are built into everything we do at Slumberkins. They're also built into our daily lives and family routines. Words have the power to build ourselves and others up or down. Speaking positive affirmations into your child's life before they can even speak for themselves is like planting the seeds of emotional well-being.
>
> —Callie

Affirmations aren't just a "nice" thing to do with your child. Research supports the idea that affirmations can bring about positive effects. The self-affirmation theory, for example, states that positive affirmations are beneficial in three ways:

Self-identity: If we consistently tell ourselves that we are smart, this positive thought becomes the narrative that we believe is true. This, in turn, helps us to take actions that reinforce this narrative, essentially becoming what we believe we are.

Self-efficacy: Affirmations help stir our consciousness and awaken us to the idea that we can do or be something better. Self-efficacy reinforces the possibility of improvement and growth by reminding us that we have control over our actions and behaviors.

Self-integrity: We want to believe that we are moral and capable of making the right decisions, even in challenging situations. This sense of self-integrity can motivate us to choose the moral option while also giving us confidence that we are capable of doing so.

So when we tell positive stories about ourselves, encourage ourselves to improve, and believe we are capable, we begin to harness the power to turn the things we *want* to be true about ourselves into things that are *actually* true about ourselves.

GROW

Growth isn't a "final step" in a linear progression. Emotional growth can be messy and uncomfortable. There will never be a moment where you have figured everything out and you've reached emotional development parenting perfection. That's the beauty and the frustration of it all.

When we engage in our children's emotional development early on, we can empower them to be more caring, confident, and resilient, helping them see every experience—pleasant or difficult—as an opportunity for growth. And that growth is never complete. We continue the process throughout our life cycle. We continue to shift and change because our lives and our relationships are dynamic. Even if you get to a point when you've done it—you've broken a cycle—and you say to yourself, "Wow, I'm so proud of the way I showed up for my child," there will still be more work to do on this emotional journey. Growth is a continual part of the process.

Make sure to take moments to celebrate the growth that comes from doing this work. Shifting into a more connected and conscious way of parenting is *hard work*, especially because most of us did not grow up in a family that knew how to approach emotional learning and development in this way. In many ways, we are all reparenting ourselves on our own personal growth journeys while parenting our children.

Think of the process as leveling up . . . but without a ceiling. Though it may feel like you've taken two steps forward and five steps back sometimes, it all collectively helps you progress.

It's worth noting that emotional intelligence doesn't necessarily equal emotional wellness. You can know all the information, but if you aren't able to believe it on a felt personal level, then you won't be able to practice what you preach. We all have different areas we need to work on, and we will all continuously have those areas to work on.

But it does get easier.

I have always been a person who is highly tuned in to other people's emotions. I was a very easy child; my mom said I "never" had any issues. (Sure, Mom!) I was a good student, top athlete, very good friend . . . and all of the things that made me "good". And now with my training, I have a superpower for supporting emotions. But that doesn't mean that internally for me everything is worked out. My pain and difficult experiences set me up with the ability to understand other people better than I understand myself sometimes.

Now, as an adult, my work is to stop focusing outward and try to tune in to myself. I am focusing on understanding my *own* feelings and needs, setting better boundaries, and making choices that feel vulnerable and scary to me. This often means meeting my own needs in moments when my past self would have chosen to keep the focus on others.

—Kelly

INCORPORATING CONNECT-TO-GROW IN YOUR DAILY LIFE

We know how stressful being a parent can be, day in and day out. The amazing news about learning to parent using this approach is that it works, and it isn't something you have to add to your list of to-dos. You can truly just integrate the approach into your existing routines.

It should not add to the mental load and lists of to-dos. Emotional learning happens 24/7 in a family system, and we are here to help you integrate this approach in the most effortless way, while you and your kids experience the benefits and emotional growth together. It can be overwhelming to think about all of the things you want to change, so showing up in small but consistent ways is key.

You might want to be the A+ student who reads this book and wants to do every single thing we suggest by the end of the week, but remember that you can't rush your healing. Take bite-size, doable steps and be conscious that sometimes things can feel worse before they get better, especially if you struggle with processing difficult emotions along the way.

We know that your daily routine and family dynamics and experiences are as varied and unique as you are. There are lots of ways to integrate this approach into your parenting routines, and even though every family has their own rhythm, we trust you will be able to take these examples and incorporate them in ways that work for you and your family.

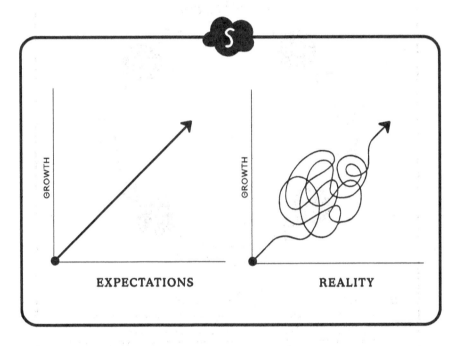

For many of us, this approach does include healing and learning new skills right along with our kids. Anytime we do something for the first time, it's going to be hard. But we can assure you that it will feel better over time. Using the Connect-to-Grow approach can supercharge recurring moments in your parenting day.

♡ CONNECT

Facilitate meaningful moments of connection that allow children to feel seen, valued, and loved at the deepest level. Allowing all feelings to be expressed in these moments of connection helps solidify the bonds that are essential for an emotionally healthy childhood.

♡ REFLECT

We apply two definitions of "reflect," the first meaning to *mirror*. Young children develop a sense of self when their parents and primary caregivers mirror and reflect back the child's feelings, responses, and actions.

The second is when children feel seen, heard, and understood by their parents, they can feel safe to engage in *self-reflection*. Parents can model self-talk, approach difficult feelings with curiosity rather than judgment, and use deep breathing or body regulation techniques to help their children internalize behavior that encourages self-reflection.

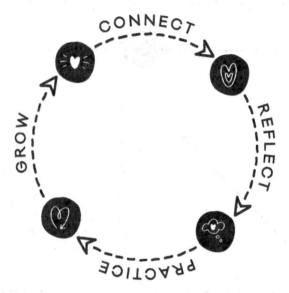

♡ GROW

Growth isn't a "final step" or linear progression. Emotional growth can be messy and uncomfortable and can start at any age. When we engage in our children's emotional development early, we can empower them to be more caring, confident, and resilient, where they see every experience—pleasant or difficult—as an opportunity for growth.

♡ PRACTICE

To reinforce the connection we have with our children, we must actively participate in the emotional growth journey. Using affirmations enhances the learning and provides children with concrete reminders of emotional skills, supporting the formation of positive core beliefs that are being learned during the moments of Connect and Reflect.

Additionally, as parents, we have the responsibility to engage in our own practice of modeling emotional skills. When children see a parent identify their emotions, acknowledge their mistakes, and practice self-awareness, they are actively learning how this translates to real-life situations through you.

Here are some typical points in the day when you might consider trying some of these strategies. You might notice that these moments are times that you may already be in connection with your children.

- Morning routine
- Pre-nap
- Driving in the car
- After school
- Bath time
- Family time
- Bedtime routine

We're going to zoom in on the bedtime routine as one of our favorite examples to be proactive with our own children. This is where we often recommend that families begin.

If you do not have a Slumberkins character book at home, don't stress. Grab your child's favorite bedtime story, and we'll walk you through how to set this up. Some of the ways you can enhance that existing routine to include therapeutic benefits are to make sure you maintain the following:

Eye contact: Do this before and after the story; it helps your little one know you are fully present.

Connected attunement: If a character shares an emotion in the story, ask your child if they have ever felt like that. Making connections to their lived experiences with them is a way for them to feel understood.

Playful interaction: If there's a funny part in the book and your child wants to act it out, let them! Children learn through play, and it'll be even more impactful if you can join them in the playful interaction, entering their world and processing the story.

Safe touch: If it's bedtime, you're probably already used to incorporating a (consented upon) hug and kiss goodnight. Adding snuggling or high fives supports your children's sense of safety, creating a sense of calm that allows them to enter into a receptive learning state.

After a few nights of adding more intentionality to your bedtime routine, reflect on the process. Do you feel more connected to your child? Does your child seem to enjoy the time you spend together? If so, continue, and add more moments of connection throughout the day. If something doesn't feel exactly right, tweak the routine. Maybe your child would rather sing a song together than read a book. Maybe you try a discussion about your "high" and "low" from the day. Or maybe your child happens to be more receptive at dinnertime than bedtime.

The beauty of this approach is that it is completely flexible to your family's needs. Nothing is prescriptive or set in stone. As you strive to connect, you will become more in tune with what your child wants from you, helping your relationship grow and flourish. So even if you have only a few spare minutes of time (and patience) each day, use that time mindfully and wisely. Get the most out of every moment.

BEFORE YOU START PART 2 . . .

Know that emotional learning can start at any age. And no matter when you start, it will always feel a little bumpy at the beginning.

That's part of the process.

When you begin the work of emotional learning and reflection, you may feel overwhelmed at times. You may feel like you "get it" one day and are totally lost the next. We know that you are doing your best. The process is never linear, but the payout is gold. You'll eventually reach a deeper state of connection to yourself and your loved ones. Through this work, you'll learn to accept and love yourself and each other, creating more empathy, compassion, and connection in your everyday life.

Focus on the tasks that make you feel good, that you enjoy. Emotional learning can be fun, deep, and meaningful . . . all at the same time. Think of it as making core memories with your kids that they will remember in their future relationships with their own children.

If you happen to have been disconnected from your kids recently (maybe that's the reason you're reading this book), they've probably found ways to keep themselves busy and not rely on your connection as much, such as through screen time, games, or playing on their own. That's a normal human response. If you want to start building these connections and supporting their emotional growth, you might need to lean in to their world at the outset. What are they interested in? How can you join them in their world? Remember, it's not important for you to learn how to play their video game. It's important for you to understand why they like playing video games. How do video games make them feel? What do they find interesting about them? When do they like to play them? By showing interest in their world and interests, you are introducing a moment of connection.

> Kids are craving connection, even if they've found ways of coping in disconnection.
>
> —Callie

As you move into Part 2 of this book and dive into the different themes or skills you think will help support your child, we encourage you to stay curious, even if you might have a different opinion, view, or belief. When we approach situations, people, feelings, or even our thoughts with curiosity, we step away from the need to protect our existing beliefs or to validate our existing stories. This shift is profound—it sets us on the path to learning and self-discovery.

Think of curiosity as the antithesis of defensiveness. A curious person does not shut off when confronted with a different perspective or a challenging situation. Instead, they lean in, eager to understand, to unravel the mystery, to find the hidden insight that might at first seem unfamiliar or even uncomfortable. At the end of the day, we want you to be open to gaining awareness of core beliefs you may not even realize you hold. Our goal is not to change you but simply to assist you in gaining a deeper understanding of yourself and your own emotional makeup in a way that will help you and your child.

In simple terms, we are asking you to put down your defenses. Consider the possibility that there is a different approach or perspective that could be helpful to you. Remember, every moment is an opportunity to learn, and curiosity is your key to unlocking these endless opportunities.

Now you just need to start the process. But as we mentioned, the word *start* can be misleading because even though you begin somewhere, there is no finish line. You're always up against an emotional growth edge. But here's the good news: if you're reading this book, if you're interested in this topic, then you've already started. If you want to show up for your kid and create a better life for them, if you want them to feel happy and connected and loved, and if you want to improve yourself along the way, you're on the path. Whether you know what you're doing or you don't know what you're doing, it's all unfolding, and it's all happening.

The goal is to slowly become more aware of what's happening—as it's happening—so you can enjoy the process of building the foundation for a lifetime of emotional wellness for your kids.

PART TWO

PUTTING IT INTO PRACTICE

CHAPTER 5

The Connect-to-Grow Approach in Practice

In this part of the book, we are going to examine the 15 core themes or skills that make up the foundation of the emotional development roadmap. In each chapter that follows, we will guide you to proactively build emotional skills and strategies that support your child, as well as make suggestions to repair if you start to see signs of perfectionism or anxiety arise.

You may see some of these icons appear throughout this book.

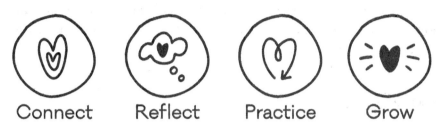

Connect   Reflect   Practice   Grow

They remind you of the Connect-to-Grow approach that is being used in each situation. For a higher-level overview of the theory that informs the approach, check out Chapter 4, "Connect-to-Grow: Breaking Down the Approach."

Even though we have divided the emotional learning roadmap into 15 chapters, the journey will not be clearcut. There's a reason that therapists often start answering questions with "It depends. . . ." From person to person, or family to family, situations are complex and nuanced. That's why we want to make sure you have a comprehensive resource at your fingertips to provide you and your family with the most effective tools and resources we have to offer.

If you're looking for a specific topic or issue that doesn't happen to be the title of one of these chapters, turn to the Use Case Table at the back of the book to find a key to the chapters you should read. Think of it as a general recommendation based on needs that a teacher or school counselor might share with families they work with.

You can read this part of the book straight through, or you can start with needs you see in your child's life currently so you can get right to work. As you start to implement our approach in your family, you may see your child's needs shift or change. Continue exploring other chapters to pinpoint the support you and your child need to continue the process.

Each of the following chapters contains an explanation of the issue and a story pulled from real life to illustrate the skill you're trying to build, plus tools, tips, affirmations, parent reflections, and actionable ideas that you can try today.

Most of the content is easy to understand and implement, but we want to take a look at two areas that may need additional explanation: CALM moments and Move Forward.

CALM MOMENTS

Each chapter is designed to help you bolster your child's emotional development, but we want to take care of you, the parent, as well. Toward the end of each chapter, we include a moment of CALM for parents, which is a thoughtful method designed to help us pause, reflect, and respond in a way that fosters understanding and growth. Since parents navigate a complex array of emotions and experiences, it's crucial to have a method to find peace within ourselves, both for our benefit and our children's benefit as well.

The CALM approach starts with Centering Yourself, allowing you to take a step back and ground yourself amidst the chaos of parenting. This initial step is about finding a moment of tranquility, allowing deep breaths to offer a pause in our busy lives.

C - Center Yourself:

Begin with slow, deep breaths. Close your eyes if it helps, placing your hands on your heart or belly. Use this moment to slow down physically and mentally. Recognize and acknowledge your feelings and any thoughts that arise.

A - Acknowledge and Reflect:

Next, we Acknowledge and Reflect. This stage is key in understanding not just what is happening around us, but also within us. Here, we delve into our emotions and thoughts, asking ourselves introspective questions. This reflective practice gives us insight into our reactions and behaviors, encouraging us to consider how our own experiences, perhaps even from childhood, shape our parenting style. (See questions for Reflection in each section.)

Find corresponding reflection questions in each chapter to focus on.

L - Listen and Act:

Then, we Listen and Act. This is where awareness transforms into action. We'll help you listen to your inner voice and the needs of your child, comparing both to decide the most nurturing course of action.

Notice what your body, emotions, thoughts, and memories are telling you. Consider what you and your family members need in this moment, especially regarding the topic of interest that you are focusing on in the corresponding chapter.

M - Move Forward with Intention:

Finally, we Move Forward with Intention. This step is about applying what we've learned through reflection and transforming it into positive change.

Decide how you want to apply these insights. This might involve creating more meaningful interactions with your child or seeking therapy and support for attachment wounds and past traumas. Think about what steps you can take to strengthen your family's connections.

When we have a chance to connect with ourselves (and our children), the process might bring forward feelings, emotions, thoughts, or beliefs that we weren't fully aware of. These insights can be so helpful in our parenting journey, but it can be tricky to know what to do with that knowledge.

If, after you read a chapter and start implementing new techniques, you have a moment of insight or clarity (whether positive or negative), don't just let that moment pass you by. Instead, take action. If the insight is positive, you will want to remember that and integrate more fully into your life. If the insight is negative, you may want to do some deeper work to turn things around.

Here are a handful of ways you may choose to keep moving forward with the work:

- Journal or reflect on what you learned.
- Seek therapy or support for healing you need.
- Speak to your partner or family members to work together on a need or a celebration.
- Take the empathy you gained from reflecting on your childhood and bring that forward into your interactions with your child.
- Find healthy ways to see your child's situation as clearly different from your own.
- Sit with and allow any big feelings (or your own grief) to be released so that you can give your child the gift of presence and support.
- Apologize to your child for your reaction to something that may have caused them harm.
- Take a moment of self-care to soothe your own emotions or find space to get your own needs met.

There are many, many directions you may choose to go in once you begin this work. Just don't stand still. You have the ability to grow and change just like your child does.

Each step of the CALM approach offers a moment to not only manage the immediate situation but also to process our experiences.

These moments are meant to be like our oxygen mask. Supporting the emotional development of our kids can be exhausting, and these moments are crucial to take care of ourselves along the way. So, even if you take a moment of CALM in your car in your driveway before going into your house, or you have to seclude yourself in your closet to even be able to have the space to reflect, we encourage you to try these and see what comes forward for you in your awareness and system. These moments help you connect to yourself and stay grounded and by putting in the time, it will open your capacity to show up in the ways you want to for your kids.

Now that you have the tools to take care of yourself and foster your own growth, let us introduce you to some sweet friends who will help you and your child on the journey.

MEET THE CHARACTERS

All of the characters in the Slumberkins universe are simply mascots of the emotional wellness skill or theme. The books are tools that you may choose to use, and the only difference between using the books and proceeding without is that the books and content make everything ready to implement into your daily parenting routine. In other words, they save you time and mental energy. However, the approach is completely available and valuable whether you use the books or not.

You'll see that certain Slumberkins characters connect to each chapter in this book. We did this to illustrate how to line up the theory and strategy with the correct character if you so choose. We have also divided the Slumberkins into three groups, or "crews," that help your child ladder up and build skills that will help make them a caring, confident, resilient kid.

We start with the **Caring Crew**, which helps children learn to take care of themselves and others. Then, we move on to the **Confidence Crew**, which fosters children's belief in themselves and their ability to face challenges. Finally, we have the **Resilience Crew**, which helps instill the belief that we can get through hard times and we don't have to do it alone.

Now let's get to know the characters within each crew.

Crew Members: Sloth, Otter, Yeti, Ibex, Honey Bear

This crew supports children in learning to take care of themselves and others.

Our early relationships define how we see and understand ourselves in the world. They set the foundations we'll use for the rest of our lives. First we have to understand ourselves, and we only understand ourselves through the eyes of other people. That's why we're relational beings. We wouldn't know who we are or what we are if we didn't have a mirror; we see ourselves through the eyes of our caregivers.

Sloth—Routines: This collection focuses on the concept of structure and routines. Through structure and routines, children find stability and safety in their environments, eventually internalizing them and gaining the skills necessary to take care of themselves. It's important for parents to actively support and model a healthy relationship to structure and flexibility. This collection supports parents in having the tools to create supportive structures and tools for their children's lives, while also reminding parents to take care of themselves.

Otter—Building Connections: This collection is all about attachment and creating safe and stable relationships first and foremost with our primary caregivers but then expanding to cultivate and connect with friends and the greater community. This helps children be prepared and well-equipped to foster belonging and connection throughout their lives.

Yeti—Mindfulness: In a world as hectic and overwhelming as ours, having the tools to help find your center or slow down in the hectic moments is essential. We believe mindfulness is one of the most important tools to have in your toolbox. If we want our kids to be able to welcome all feelings and be resilient in the face of challenges, the ability to find presence is essential. The process of consciously practicing mindfulness is a tool that is highly beneficial for adults as well as children. This collection gives the tools for both parent and child to learn how to tune in to their senses, thoughts, and feelings so that both can work on mindfulness techniques together.

Ibex—Emotional Courage: This collection focuses on identifying and welcoming all feelings. This concept is crucial to start a foundation of emotional intelligence. In a world that tells us that feelings are "weak" or some feelings are "bad," we want to help parents reframe the narrative. To understand ourselves and others better, we must accept and hold space for all the messages that our feelings tell us. This is true courage and the basis of strong emotional intelligence. We believe that these skills will be the most important skills a person can have in the future.

Honey Bear—Gratitude: This collection focuses on another tool that we see as an essential for any parent and child on their journey through life. Gratitude is a powerful emotion and can be used to cultivate a practice that sets people up to feel fulfilled and abundant in their lives. By helping a child understand the powerful feeling of gratitude through their relationship with their parent and by encouraging moments of mindfulness to notice when that feeling is present, our hope is that children and adults will notice that in the present moment, there are gifts all around. When we feel gratitude, it spreads, and the outcome is more compassion, for each other and for the earth.

Crew Members: Bigfoot, Unicorn, Narwhal, Yak, Hammerhead

This crew reinforces children's belief in themselves and their ability to face challenges.

It builds on empathy, of our connection and understanding of ourselves and others, in a more complex way. A child with confidence might think, "I have feelings. These feelings are making me into something unique and different from other people, and I'm going to continue to figure out who I am, connect with other people, and do the things in the world that I feel the desire to do."

Bigfoot—Self-Esteem: At its core, self-esteem is often built on the concept of lovability, which is usually forged in our relationship with our primary caregivers. This is why we wanted to give parents the tools to make sure their child knows that they are lovable—no matter what. This collection focuses on separating our behavior or other people's ideas about us from our innate being that is *us*. The "me" in there is innately lovable—everything else is just learning. With this baseline of understanding, children cultivate a solid foundation that feelings of self-esteem can flourish from.

Unicorn—Authenticity: Authenticity is about showing up with your true personality, values, culture, identity, and spirit even in the face of pressure to act otherwise. It's only when we show up as our true selves that we can feel the full experience of unconditional love. Being able to show up authentically does come from a place of privilege, unfortunately. There are many individuals and groups for whom it is unsafe to be their authentic selves as it may pose emotional or physical danger for them. At Slumberkins, we believe it's important that we continue to work toward a world where it is safe for everyone to be their true, authentic selves.

Narwhal—Growth Mindset: If you have a growth mindset, you see challenges as opportunities to grow, and you work hard to meet the goals you set for yourself. It also suggests that intelligence comes from working hard and practicing, as opposed to being born with specific, fixed intelligence. Supporting children in building beliefs that are in alignment with a growth mindset can help them build the skills that make up grit, tenacity, and determination.

Yak—Self-Acceptance: Yak helps kids believe they are good enough just the way they are. We can always have room to learn and grow, and we don't have to be perfect to know that we are worthy of love. When we know that we are enough, we know we don't have to do or *be* anything other than ourselves to be loved and accepted. When this message starts in early childhood and is supported by a parent, a child gains the capacity to build on this concept through a lifetime, ideally staving off difficult traits like perfectionism.

Hammerhead—Conflict Resolution: Conflict resolution for children is dependent on a child's cognitive development, emotional regulation skills, and problem-solving skills. The expression of anger can be overwhelming, both for those experiencing it and for those around people experiencing it. Because of the nature of aggression and anger, it is easy for this feeling to be labeled as "bad." For children who struggle with big feelings, they can quickly get the message that they are bad if they feel mad. This collection focuses on righting that message by helping parents and kids see that anger carries an important message, and we need to work together to understand what it's telling us.

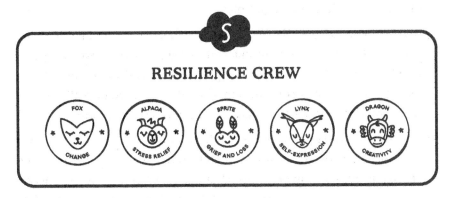

Crew Members: Fox, Alpaca, Sprite, Lynx, Dragon

This crew reminds us all that we can get through hard times, and we don't have to do it alone.

There will be moments that are going to come and try to run you off the road. No matter what happens, you can't avoid them. Everyone is going to experience disappointment. Everyone is going to experience grief and loss. That's just part of living. Resilience includes all the things you lean on when life feels out of your control.

Fox—Change: Change can mean a lot of different things. It could be a small change like a change in schedule or routine, the need to buy a bigger set of clothes, or a move to a new home. Change could also be something big in the family like a death of a loved one or a divorce. Some changes are good, some are not good, and some are a mix of both. Regardless, change of any kind can be hard for people. Big life changes are often out of the control of even the parent or caregiver. Ensuring that change is not a child's fault can increase trust and attachment and help a child process big feelings.

Alpaca—Anxiety: The Stress Relief collection was created to support children and families in times of stress, anxiety, and worry. When life gets tough, we need resilience and support to help us understand that we can get through tough times—and we don't have to do it alone. We can lean on others to help us in tough times.

Sprite—Grief and Loss: There is no "getting over" grief, and it's not a linear process. Grief is not only attached to death. There are many types of grief and loss, like a move, growing up, or a friendship ending. While feelings of grief are normal, the emotions it creates can be really big, but there are many ways that we can help our kids cope with loss.

Lynx—Self-Expression: We want children to trust their inner voice and share their perspectives with safe adults and community members. We also really want to help kids learn about healthy boundaries and consent at an early age. Helping empower children with a strong voice and an understanding of their boundaries, both emotional and physical, helps guard them against those who might take advantage of them.

Dragon—Creativity: Creativity refers to the ability to generate or discover new ideas, solutions, and possibilities in just about any field, topic, or activity. Creativity is about tapping into our own imagination, curiosity, and interests. It has been shown to reduce anxiety, increase coping skills, and bring meaning and accomplishment into people's lives. When we have the open door to find and tap into our creativity, it can be a powerful tool for healing.

Now that you have a high-level understanding of how this part of the book is structured, let's dive into each theme and get to work.

CHAPTER 6

Routines

M any of us operate differently in our day-to-day lives. There are morning people and night people. There are those who love organization and those who hate it. Some of us may thrive in unstructured environments, and others may cling to structure and routines as their daily lifesaver.

If you're the type who depends on your routines, we see you and feel you.

As educators, we know structure is key to setting students up to manage themselves in the classroom and throughout their day. Students have so many things to juggle while taking in tons of new information and navigating the social-emotional aspect of the classroom and school environment. A predictable schedule and plan can make children feel safe; they like to know what to expect.

As a parent, if you're the type who prefers less structure to your day, you may be more spontaneous and have an openness to whatever comes your way as you go. However spontaneous you are, you likely have some things in your day that you can rely on. Predictability around portions of your day can help you feel organized and safe, which allows you to feel grounded and lean into more unpredictable moments. This is important to recognize because no matter how you feel about routines, they are an important topic when it comes to parenting.

Obviously, there is no one right way to raise a child. It all comes down to a balance between structure and flexibility. After all, we can have the best plan mapped out, but if our toddler decides it's time for a tantrum while trying to get out the door, we need to be able to adapt without it completely ruining our day. Or vice versa, you might be a flexible and on-the-go type of person but find that you have a very crabby toddler if you haven't planned some downtime or snack breaks.

From a therapeutic lens, the benefits of structure and routine in a child's life cannot be ignored—even for the free spirits among you. They help a child form the positive core belief that they are cared for and loved by their primary caregiver.

WHY ROUTINES ARE SO IMPORTANT

Routines are extremely important for infants and children. Having consistent daily routines helps children develop a sense of safety and confidence in knowing what comes next. The predictability of the day helps them feel safe and secure. Routines can be individualized for each family, especially since they need to be set up to meet the needs of all family members. Children can learn to be part of their regular routines and will eventually learn to care more and more for themselves. This is an important part of child development.

ROUTINES THROUGH THE AGES

At first, parents can tune in to the regular rhythms of their babies, but after a few months, parents can support a routine by setting a general schedule around meals, sleep, and play. Routines help support babies by building a foundation of secure attachment and feelings of safety and security in their ability to predict what comes next in their days. Bedtime routines, specifically, help babies tune in to sleep cues that promote rest. Having a balance between routines and flexibility will help serve your family's needs.

Toddlers and little kids also love knowing what comes next. Routines become a foundation for growing independence. Preschoolers may begin to dress themselves, brush their teeth, and get their shoes on in the morning if they know the routine and expectations. Knowing what is coming next and what the expectations are of them can help them feel calm. This can be really helpful if you notice that your little one is more wired to be worried or is feeling stressed for whatever reason.

Big kids may benefit from a bit of flexibility, so allow them the chance to show more independence with their routines. More and more kids can learn to care for themselves at this age, which is an important part of learning routines. Big kids can start to understand their own needs and use routines and structure to support themselves, little by little.

Both Kelly and I tend to operate just fine with a less structured day. We are both free spirits and love to spontaneously drop everything if one of us has an idea that sounds fun. We love fun, we love to enjoy life, and we think it's all just one big adventure. Well, that approach to living life with new babies and very little sleep can send you into a unhealthy downward spiral. If you're anything like us, you might even go off the rails and not even see the crash coming: you just wake up one day and realize you're in trouble. Your fuel gauge is on Empty. You've hit burnout.

When we lack routine and neglect self-care, Kelly and I reach our maximum capacity for chaos, and we have to get ourselves back to a baseline. When those moments occur, they're like an emergency, and it's time for us to put our oxygen masks on first to save ourselves and then check on our families.

As parents, it can be easier in the short term to convince ourselves that our kids' needs come first. But we've experienced that it's much more problematic if you get to the point that you can't care for yourself or your child. We've each hit that edge and needed to turn some serious attention to our own routines and structure to manage the demands of daily life and parenting.

Structure has become less of a "nice idea" and more of an "everyday core need" to thrive. When we translate this to our children's experiences, we know it's essential rather than optional.

—Callie

For routines, the core beliefs that are forming are the concepts of safety and autonomy.

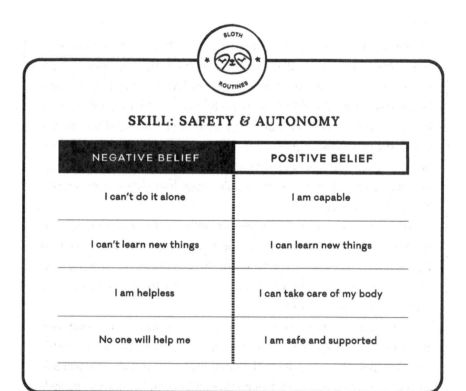

SKILL: SAFETY & AUTONOMY

NEGATIVE BELIEF	POSITIVE BELIEF
I can't do it alone	I am capable
I can't learn new things	I can learn new things
I am helpless	I can take care of my body
No one will help me	I am safe and supported

When it comes to safety and autonomy, there are two concepts we want our kids learn:

- Routines and structure are there to keep us safe.
- They can learn skills to take care of themselves over time.

Even if you lived the first 30 years of your life as a free spirit who never wore a watch or meal planned a day in your life, you will likely have to introduce some structure and routine into your life when you become a parent. Lack of structure in early childhood can impact the development of core beliefs like these:

Security and trust: Structure and routine provide a sense of predictability and safety for children. Kids thrive on knowing when they'll eat and when they're expected to sleep. So much of their world is new and unfamiliar that they find reassurance in the rhythms of the day. Without a routine, children may come to view the world as unpredictable and chaotic, leading to anxiety and difficulty in forming secure attachments later in life.

Self-esteem and self-efficacy: When you set limits, you give kids a structured container that helps them learn about their environment, achieve their goals, and understand their abilities. In the absence of limits, children might struggle to develop a sense of competence and self-efficacy.

Control and autonomy: Structure teaches children that their actions have consequences and that they have some control over their outcomes. Without structure, they may start to believe that they are powerless or lack autonomy, leading to risk-taking behaviors in the future.

Social norms and relationships: Early childhood structure often includes learning social norms, boundaries, and interactions with others. Without structure, kids may think they do not fit in or may have trouble forming healthy relationships.

Resilience and coping skills: Structured environments help kids build resilience by providing them with challenges and giving them the tools to overcome them. Building this muscle helps children handle stress and adversity later in life.

Although structure and routines are essential for all the reasons we just outlined, it should be balanced with opportunities for free play and exploration, which are also crucial for healthy development. The key is to provide an environment where children feel safe and supported but are also encouraged to learn, explore, and grow.

PROACTIVELY SETTING UP ROUTINES AND STRUCTURE

Let's take a closer look at how—and why—to set up routines and structure based on the age of your child. You can see that some of the suggestions are fairly similar through the ages, but others differ as children age.

Incorporating these routines should be done with flexibility, especially as infants often need adjustments based on their growth and development stages. The key is to gradually introduce a sense of regularity in a way that is responsive to your infant's needs.

For babies, a consistent sleep routine is essential (also for your sanity!) Equally, predictable feeding times. Although very young infants may need to be fed on demand, you can gradually introduce more predictable feeding times as they grow. It's also important to have regular play and interaction times. Set aside time each day for activities like tummy time, reading aloud (even to an infant), or simply talking and singing to your baby. This not only aids in bonding but also establishes a routine that contributes to their cognitive and emotional development.

Little kids (toddlers) thrive on predictability, and knowing what to expect helps them feel secure. Meltdowns may occur when toddlers feel out of control, so keeping to the routine can help keep the peace. A consistent bedtime routine—such as a bedtime story—is also important to establish and maintain, as are regular times for meals and snacks. Regular play and learning is essential at this stage, too. Schedule regular times for play and educational activities to boost their cognitive and motor skill development. Be consistent but also prepare to adjust the routine as needed, and allow your child opportunities to cultivate independence by making small choices, such as choosing a book to read. And of course, allow for downtime.

With older kids, consistent morning and evening routines are very important. Activities like getting dressed, eating breakfast, and packing their backpacks prepare them for their day, while evening routines like doing homework, having dinner, and reading help them wind down. Participation in extracurricular activities provide structure and social interaction, but make sure their schedule isn't too jam-packed. To encourage responsibility, assign age-appropriate chores and responsibilities, such as making beds, tidying bedrooms, or helping with simple tasks. And family time—game nights, family meals—are key to forming close connections with older kids.

SUPPORTING EMERGING INDEPENDENCE

Supporting children with routines is about empowering children to move toward more and more independence. This means that although we as parents start out creating the routines, as our children become capable, we can allow and encourage them to explore and do more and more on their own. For example, allow your child to pick out what they are going to wear within their morning routine, or pick out the book at bedtime.

As children get older, they may have ideas about how certain routines could change. Being able to be flexible and stay connected to the reason we are using these routines (to empower a feeling of safety and the ability to be independent) can be helpful for parents who have a harder time letting the routines and structures change. Remember, being too rigid about routine and structure can have the opposite effect you are looking for and actually hurt independence. Too much structure can support a belief that they can't do things on their own and that they aren't capable. It's always a balancing act of supporting structure while also leaving room for growth and flexibility.

AFFIRMATION

When we have a routine,
I know what to do.
I am cared for
and loved by me and you.

THE BEDTIME ROUTINE: IMPLEMENTING STRUCTURE AND TOOLS TO SUPPORT THE PROCESS

Often, when you first tell someone becoming a parent, one of the first comments you'll hear is "You'll never sleep again!"

And once the baby is born, you'll hear "How's the baby sleeping? How are you sleeping?"

Like us, you may have experienced uncomfortable nights during your pregnancy when you're not getting the deepest sleep. You may have been hoping to catch up once the baby was born. (Newborns sleep a lot of hours each day, right?) But then you became a parent and sleep was an even scarcer resource (because of course those hours of sleep are never *in a row*).

Sleep becomes a hot topic for parents and kids in the early years. Until you have experienced the lack of sleep that comes with early parenting, you can't truly appreciate how incredible a good night of sleep can be. But we won't get good sleep unless our kids are also getting good sleep.

We aren't going to pretend to be sleep experts. There are many books and experts who will be able to guide you in your path to finding out what works for you and your child. The tactics and logistics you choose to approach sleep are up to you. But what we are experts at is infusing therapeutic techniques into everyday parenting moments. As moms, we knew that the most connected moments we spent with our kids usually happened during the bedtime routine. That's why we encourage parents to use research-backed techniques as part of the bedtime routine toolbox.

With that in mind, we wanted to infuse a bedtime routine with methods that support your child in becoming more autonomous in getting to sleep. Part of the process of getting your child to bed requires getting them to slow down and start relaxing. The problem is that young children are so full of energy and wonder that they have a hard time making the transition from playtime to relaxation. They usually play so hard that sleep will just sneak up on them—they are not consciously calming down; they're just passing out.

Part of what we are helping our children do when we create routines around bedtime is guiding them to consciously seek the rest they so desperately need. Some days are rainy and kids don't get to let off all their steam and run around the playground for hours, so they might not go to sleep quickly at bedtime. If you think about it, this is part of what becomes hard about sleep for adults as well. We have to plan and balance our schedules to help our bodies get the balance of activity and rest we need so that we can engage in all the mental and physical activities we have planned for the next day. As we grow, structure and routine become very important so we can manage our lives and do the whole "adulting" thing.

Your Child's Need for Sleep

Newborns emerge from an environment that has no circadian rhythm. They were part of your body, and they were affected by your movement, but not by other humans.

After babies enter the world, they're introduced to their own senses and an environment that's full of stimuli—pain, cold, heat—and they're really getting exposed to the elements. At that point, sleep becomes a place of respite. While they sleep, babies' brains process a great deal of essential mental and emotional growth. This is why babies sleep so much—they really need those moments of processing for their regulation.

Especially for kids in the early years, giving structure, routines, cues, clues leading up to moments that you're looking to promote, like sleep, is really important. Your role is to basically set up the conditions and the routines that can be counted on to help transition children into their sleeping times. As you do so, those moments become more and more predictable—and emotionally, kids can feel the security and the safety of knowing what's coming. Think about things like sleep hygiene, low lighting, and a quiet environment to help get your child in a place where they can fall asleep on their own. Whatever that routine ends up being for your family is the signal that it's time to wind down.

For babies and younger kids, you can say something like "We're getting into our cozy spot. This is how we calm our bodies down." For older kids, we created a progressive muscle relaxation routine to help them tune in to their bodies and reduce tension.

When you lead your kids through structure and routine, you are showing them how those things create safety, suggest predictability, build confidence, and improve their way of functioning in the world. Keep in mind that as kids' developmental needs change, they can participate more fully in the routine, which may mean that the routine itself changes a bit. Over time, those external structures become internalized; they're something kids can use to balance the unpredictability of other aspects of their lives, and they can continue to build on that foundation.

Your role is really to create those moments according to what feels right to you. There's not one way to do it. People have different setups, they have different sleeping arrangements, and they have different values about quality time, family time, how long they sleep, and what they do during the day. What we promote is that you should tune in to what is right for your family in creating the structure and routines that work for you.

Just be careful of relying on these routines to put your child to sleep *for* you.

The thing I love most about using the *Sloth Starts to Slumber* book at bedtime with my own kids is how it's interactive in a way that facilitates meaningful connection. It quickly became my kids' favorite bedtime story. While they are reaping the benefits of my presence, attunement, and interaction—all things that help build the positive attachments that we know are foundational to a child's emotional health—they love it, and it's easy for me. Reading the book takes all of five minutes, and I feel like a better mom when I know they're getting those present moments in a fun and routine way.

There have been so many times where someone will say, "I don't know what you did to these Slumberkins snugglers. Maybe you use magic fairy dust or something, but my child is obsessed with it!" And while we are always so thrilled and honored to hear that kids genuinely love and cherish them, there's actually nothing extra special about the plush itself.

The magic comes from a different source. The plush character is a physical representation of the meaningful moments of connection that our kids crave and need from us as parents. They love the character because it represents the times they feel most seen and supported by you. *You* are the magic.

This is what we mean when we say Slumberkins helps build positive attachments: through using the books with the plush to help facilitate, build, and solidify bonds in the early years of your child's life.

—Callie

AFFIRMATION

I go to sleep.
I snooze and slumber.
I crawl into bed and
have dreams full of wonder.

PARENT REFLECTION MOMENT: ROUTINES

Whether you are feeling overly busy or a bit understimulated, it's always great to check in with yourself about how your daily routines feel. Perhaps your schedule is overloaded with care for others; maybe it's time to make sure that self-care is included in your daily plan. Wherever you are in your process, remember that routines always need to be re-examined. The same routine rarely will work forever. Here are some questions to consider if you would like to implement our CALM Moment with a focus on Routines. You can return to Chapter 5, pages 98–100 ("CALM Moments") to have an outline of this process as you engage in the following Reflection Questions.

In moments of struggle, when seeking clarity and self-comfort, ponder these questions:

- What are my needs at this moment that aren't getting met?
- What needs do my family members have right now that aren't getting met?

If you want to reflect on your routines in general, try asking yourself:

- What is one thing I can do to take care of myself today?
- Am I getting what I need with my daily routine? Is my child or family getting what they need from their daily routine?

Things to Remember

- Structure and routines—and sleep!—are as important for you as a parent as they are for your child.
- Consistency in routine will help your child feel safe and secure.
- Give your child tools to help kids take care of their own needs (sleep, hygiene, getting dressed). This builds confidence and encourages gradual autonomy.
- If you need a routine reset, make the change gradually.
- A balance of structure and flexibility is the goal. If you are more drawn to routines, find ways to incorporate unstructured time. If you struggle implementing routines, try to find more structure. Find the happy medium, and remember, it's always a moving target.

SLUMBERKINS CHARACTER CONNECTION: SLOTH

CHAPTER 7

Building Connections

Have you ever felt like you don't belong? Belonging, at its core, is the experience of being part of something larger than ourselves, where we are accepted, valued, and understood. This fundamental human need plays a critical role in shaping our emotional well-being.

Relationships provide us with a sense of security and support, serving as a buffer against life's challenges and stressors. In moments of difficulty, knowing we have a network of support can be a source of immense comfort and strength. The feeling of being part of a community fosters a sense of purpose and belonging, which is essential for our overall happiness and satisfaction in life.

WHY CONNECTIONS ARE SO IMPORTANT

In the early 1990s research around belonging emerged as an important topic. Roy Baumeister and Mark Leary are widely seen as the pioneers of belonging research, which has been carried on and expanded by many others including renowned researcher Brené Brown. This research has highlighted that the human mind has a basic and universal drive to form and maintain relationships with other people. While this may seem obvious, a person can struggle with a sense of belonging even in loving family units. There have been studies that have shown that individuals who feel a strong sense of connection to others tend to have lower levels of anxiety and depression, higher self-esteem, and a more optimistic outlook on life. They're better able to manage anxiety and stress, and they're more resilient overall.

When we take a look at a child's emotional development and well-being, belonging serves as the emotional foundation that supports a child's mental, physical, social, and cognitive growth. When children feel they belong, they experience a deep-seated assurance of being valued and accepted within their family, school, and community.

Belonging might be important, but it's not always easy. To feel like we belong, we must first learn how to build connections with others.

While many of us start with these deep and safe connections being our family, this is not always the case. Unforeseen circumstances, mental health issues, family trauma, and large-scale events (COVID-19, war, natural disasters) turn our worlds upside down in an instant, making our once set feeling of belonging within our family feel less secure. There are less extreme versions of family events that can rupture our feeling of belonging, as well. Sibling dynamics, divorce, or blended families may upend our sense of belonging. When this happens, we seek to stay connected in new ways or find belonging in alternate environments.

The CDC-Kaiser Permanente adverse childhood experiences study helped us understand protective factors that can support long-term resilience in children. When we have even one example of a safe and connected adult and that person gives us tools to extend that feeling of security into our lives, the impact can be profound and long lasting, especially in times of stress and need. A child who lacks the feeling of belonging in their home environment may find it through a friend who becomes like family, a grandparent who always follows through on promises, a teacher who goes the extra mile, a foster family that provides a loving and safe environment, or a mentor or a coach who provides consistent guidance and support.

HOW CHILDREN LEARN TO CONNECT

In the early years, kids will be focused on their immediate families, but we know that will shift over time. (Just ask any parent with a teenager who spends more time with their friends than with them!) It is vital to help kids understand how to build meaningful connections or relationships with others so that as they start to move independently into the world, they can build upon that foundation and make good decisions about finding a sense of belonging outside of the family.

First, explicitly focus on strengthening and extending healthy bonds and *belonging* between you and your child, while discussing how to extend those bonds to "chosen family" (heart family) as they grow. (We'll talk more about Heart Families in just a bit.)

Then, help your child expand their connection with a larger community.

In fostering this sense of belonging in children, you lay the groundwork for their long-term mental health. Simple acts like spending quality family time, encouraging friendships, participating in community activities, and showing empathy and understanding in daily interactions can significantly impact their sense of belonging. It's about creating an environment where your children feel safe to express themselves, share their thoughts and feelings, have those thoughts and feelings validated by their inner circle, and know they are an integral part of your family and community.

As parents and caregivers, it's vital to model these behaviors. Showing openness in our relationships, actively listening, and being present in interactions not only strengthens our bonds but also teaches children the value of meaningful connections. Encouraging them to engage in group activities, whether in school, sports teams, or local clubs, further nurtures this sense of belonging and teaches them the importance of community.

The pursuit of belonging is not just a quest for companionship but a fundamental aspect of emotional health and wellness. By fostering a sense of belonging in our children and in ourselves, we build a foundation for lasting mental health, resilience, and happiness.

We both have personal experiences in our families that informed our decision to make a collection that supports building connections and, a sense of belonging. We wanted to create the concept of a "Heart Family," which emphasizes that whether near or far, we carry our families in our hearts. We wanted to normalize diversity within families and the importance of love, not blood, binding families together. It's so important for adults to empower children to take a fluid and positive view of the important relationships that shape their lives.

The Heart Family concept lets you define who your family is—it puts the power back in a child's hands and heart for who they feel connected to and safe enough to trust. There can be layers to the Heart Family: the inner circle, friends or classmates, and then the larger community. Being able to illustrate the bigger picture of how kids belong is so important for a child who is struggling to find their footing.

—Callie and Kelly

When we think about the skills that make up healthy connections and a sense of belonging, there are two concepts we want children to understand:

- They belong and will always be loved.
- No matter the distance or situation, they are connected to the ones they love.

For building connections, the core belief that is being formed is the concept of belonging.

SKILL: BUILDING CONNECTIONS

NEGATIVE BELIEF	POSITIVE BELIEF
I am alone	I'm always connected to the people I love
I am unloved	I am lovable
I don't belong here	I belong
Nobody cares about me	I am connected

PROACTIVELY PROMOTING A SENSE OF BELONGING AND BUILDING CONNECTIONS

Building connections is all about attachment. As we discussed in Chapter 2, "Stages of Emotional Development," *attachment* refers to a deep and enduring emotional bond that connects one person to another across time and space. Developing a "healthy" or "secure" attachment is everything in terms of predicting positive outcomes for children.

To build a baby's sense of belonging, you should build your own Heart Family. Bring your closest friends into a relationship with your child in ways that feel positive and supportive, especially in the early days. Having a community of safe and loving people to interact with you around your child, showing concern, playing with them, or even just having a tea together while your baby sleeps shows that you have healthy connections and use those connections to make your life richer.

Talking with little kids about who they love (and why) is a great place to start when introducing the concept of Heart Families. You can tell them that our hearts are special and that there is always room for more love. Help your child identify the people or animals they love. The focus on helping your child notice and be connected to your heart family network is the first step in helping them to start to understand how to build relationships and community as they grow.

Once your older child begins navigating environments outside of just the home (like school), they start to come into contact with many new people, tiptoeing into the process of creating and finding belonging in new spaces. It can be very powerful to honor and show interest in your child's chosen friend groups. Helping support positive friendships can set the stage for children to understand how to build their social groups over time.

Most of us didn't grow up with these concepts or ways of thinking about family and belonging. But that doesn't mean we all missed out on these important bonds. Close your eyes and imagine someone who helped you feel safe and cared for as a child. Chances are, the care you felt wasn't because of some fancy vacation or amazing birthday gift. You probably felt safe with them because they *saw* you during small, everyday moments—because they spent time with you and helped guide you through the unique challenges of growing up.

You can be that presence in your child's life through connecting and bonding. Whether you're celebrating a special day together or walking through the mundane moments of life, spending quality time together can help form a sense of belonging and strong connection.

EXAMPLES OF HEALTHY BONDING

Healthy bonding with your child can unfold at a moment's notice. Keep your eyes open for the moments your child might express themselves or discover a topic that interests them. These are the moments when family bonding and healthy family traditions can occur.

Healthy bonding involves fostering secure attachment through consistent positive experiences, allowing babies to trust caregivers and develop secure relationships. Supporting a child's authentic self is crucial, creating an environment where they feel safe to be themselves without fear of judgment or rejection. Spending quality time together encourages lasting connections; whether through routines like family dinners or playful moments, these interactions strengthen family bonds.

Repairing strained relationships by owning mistakes and demonstrating accountability fosters healing and teaches children valuable relationship skills. Additionally, nurturing bonds within your Heart Family—a chosen support network—provides essential support, love, and recognition for both you and your child.

Family Bonding Opportunities

Now that we've covered some of the qualities of healthy family bonding—and how it can benefit your child—let's explore some natural moments to nurture those connections.

You can strengthen your relationship with your child by sharing "big feelings" moments, which can provide an important opportunity for you to connect with your child. Sharing about yourself is another way to strengthen your relationship. Many children love to hear stories from their caregivers' childhoods.

You can also designate family bonding times. When our lives become hectic, it can feel hard to strike up spontaneous family connection and bonding moments. It helps to build proactive time into your everyday schedule.

AFFIRMATION

I am safe, I am loved.
Our connection is strong.
I have always been wanted.
I always belong.

As a parent, navigating the emotional landscape of family changes with my children has been challenging. My children have experienced some significant losses in their short lives. Otter, affectionately known as "Ottie" in our home, holds a special place in our hearts for supporting us through family changes, particularly for my youngest son.

As Callie and I created Slumberkins, there came a point where the workload was so intense that my partner and I decided that we needed help. Our parents were getting older so couldn't help out as much, and the cost of a nanny was too expensive for our budget. Because my partner spoke Spanish and we had already decided to raise our children bilingual, we looked into the option of an au pair.

The bond my children developed with Carolina was nothing short of familial. For two years she lived with us, becoming an integral part of our daily lives and a beloved member of our family. In our household, she lovingly took on the role of "Madrina" (Godmother) to my children, a title that signified the depth of our connection. When the time came for Carolina to return to her home country of Mexico, the separation was particularly hard on my youngest son. He had formed a profound attachment to her, and her departure left a noticeable void.

During this period of change, Ottie became more than just a toy; it transformed into a symbol of enduring love and connection. We had already introduced the story of the Heart Family when Carolina first came to live with us. When she had to leave, we used the concept of a Heart Family to help my son understand and cope with her absence. Carolina took an Otter with her, and my son kept his. This shared token between them served as a comforting reminder that, though physically apart, Carolina would always be part of our Heart Family.

—Kelly

RECOGNIZING IF YOUR CHILD IS STRUGGLING

Understanding the layers of connection and belonging that extends beyond your family is important, even if your immediate family is a traditional one. While some situations like the ones outlined previously more obviously need a little extra support and attention, others may be harder to spot. Some things to watch out for are:

Withdrawal from social situations: If a child frequently withdraws from interacting with family or peers or avoids group activities, it may indicate they do not feel like they belong or are part of the group.

Low self-esteem: Children who lack a sense of belonging might express feelings of worthlessness or inadequacy. They may speak negatively about themselves or believe they are not as good as others.

Behavioral changes: Look for changes in behavior such as increased irritability, aggression, or moodiness. These can be signs of frustration stemming from not feeling accepted or connected to others.

Difficulty in making friends: Struggling to make or maintain friendships can be a sign that a child doesn't feel like they belong. They may feel different from their peers or unable to connect on a deeper level.

Expressing feelings of loneliness: A child might directly express that they feel lonely or say they feel like they don't fit in anywhere.

Physical symptoms: Emotional distress from feeling like an outsider can manifest in physical symptoms like stomachaches, headaches, or a general decline in physical health.

If you notice these signs, it's important to talk to your child and understand their feelings. Providing a supportive and understanding environment at home, encouraging open communication, and possibly seeking the help of a counselor or therapist can be effective ways to help your child develop a stronger sense of belonging.

AFFIRMATION

I am connected and loved,
even if we are far apart.
I'll keep you with me,
held here in my heart.

PARENT REFLECTION MOMENT: BUILDING CONNECTIONS

There may be moments where you sense you need more connection or a sense of belonging in your own life. There may be moments when you feel a disconnect between you and your child. Perhaps you feel so angry at them that you want to disconnect; perhaps you feel like you don't have much in common sometimes. Or maybe you feel like you want a relationship with them and they are disconnecting from you or withdrawing. Remember that none of this is purposeful, and if you are feeling a disconnect of some sort, for whatever reason, this is a great moment to check in with your own heart and find ways to soothe your own system and meet your own needs before moving forward with your child. Here are some questions to consider if you would like to implement our CALM Moment with a focus on Building Connections. You can return to Chapter 5, pages 98–100 ("CALM Moments") to have an outline of this process as you engage in the following Reflection Questions.

In moments of struggle, when seeking clarity and self-comfort, ponder these questions:

- "What does this situation remind me of? Am I projecting feelings from my past onto my relationship with my child?" and "What do I need right now to soothe myself?"

For ongoing support in Building Connections:

- "What are my beliefs about relationships and where did they come from?"

- Think about someone who positively impacted you in your community when you were younger and consider, "How can I foster similar positive connections for my child?"

Things to Remember
- Building a sense of belonging is one of the most important aspects of emotional health.
- Teaching children to identify and build their own Heart Families helps foster a sense of belonging that can be built upon for a lifetime.
- A Heart Family does not have to include members of a child's biological family.
- In cases of adoption, foster care, military deployments, and divorce, building connections and belonging can make a significant impact and support children on an emotional level.

SLUMBERKINS CHARACTER CONNECTION: OTTER

CHAPTER 8

Mindfulness

Life is constantly pulling us (and our thoughts) in a thousand different directions. As adults, we often worry about the future or the past, usually without even realizing it. We are constantly analyzing or being swept up in the emotions of the "could have/should have/what if." When we focus on the future or the past, feelings of anxiety, depression, separation, and loneliness can increase, while our connection to the present fades away. This is why practicing mindfulness, which helps us stay in the present, can serve to mercifully save us—from ourselves.

Mindfulness is the practice of maintaining a nonjudgmental state of heightened or complete awareness of your thoughts, emotions, or experiences on a moment-to-moment basis. Mindfulness for kids and caregivers has been used to reduce stress, increase focus, regulate emotions, and much, much more. When we are analyzing how we could have done something better or thinking about our to-do list for tomorrow, it can feel impossible to be in a state of mindfulness. The more we practice, the easier it gets, and it is never too late or too early to start.

WHY MINDFULNESS IS SO IMPORTANT

When practicing mindfulness, we slow down and use all of our senses to pay attention to what is happening right now and accept it without judgment. When we are practicing mindfulness, we get access to presence and the present moment. There is a different quality to moments when we are able to tune in to them. There are so many ways our minds, bodies, and world pull us away from the present moment, so we constantly need to keep resetting and practicing.

In many ways, our children come into this world fully present. This is why seeing the world through their eyes is so beautiful. We remember the time when our brains didn't hold so much information, when everything just *was* and we were blissfully unaware of all of the stress and stories going on around us. If you as an adult haven't worked on this mindfulness skill yet, beginning the journey alongside your children can be a great place to start. It will be beneficial to you both. We see mindfulness as a superpower that will allow you to come back to the universal truths that ground you in moments of difficulty and dysregulation. It's the tool we want everyone to have in their toolkit and the practice that will add benefits to your emotional well-being in your everyday life.

There is so much research on mindfulness that has shown its positive benefits. Professor emeritus Jon Kabat-Zinn, founder and former director of the Stress Reduction Clinic at the University of Massachusetts Medical Center, brought the concept of mindfulness to mainstream medicine in the early 1980s. His work and others' continued research has helped to highlight that practicing mindfulness can bring improvements in both physical and psychological symptoms as well as positive changes in health, attitudes, and behaviors.

Mindfulness can be thoughtfully nurtured in our children through each stage of their psychosocial development. This is more than a practice; it's a foundational tool we can offer our children, equipping them with a resource that enriches their entire life journey. In the early years, we lay the groundwork by creating a calm and responsive environment, mirroring and validating their emotions, which teaches them to recognize and understand their feelings. As they grow into toddlers and preschoolers, introducing simple mindfulness practices like deep breathing during moments of frustration, or paying attention to the sensations while playing, can help them become more aware of their bodies and emotions.

NURTURING MINDFULNESS IN CHILDREN

Each phase of a child's development offers a unique opportunity for growth. By integrating mindfulness into each stage, we empower them with a skill that promotes emotional resilience, empathy, and a deeper understanding of themselves and the world around them.

Babies are a great reminder for how to be fully present. They are living in the moment! They don't know any other way to be. This is a beautiful time to join them and notice all the wonder that is present when you slow down.

Toddlers are still pretty inward focused, too. They don't quite yet grasp that they have autonomy or control over their internal state and are still very much in the present moment. Because this is a stage where they are starting to express themselves with language, we can help them understand their senses by labeling them. This can help to lay the foundation for greater self-understanding.

Once kids get past kindergarten, they start understanding that they have some control over their internal and external worlds. They may already be finding ways to tune in and out of the present moment. These days, some kids are able to tune in to shows, games, and virtual worlds at this very young age.

I spent time with many overstimulated kids whose parents signed them up for my mindfulness groups when I worked as a school counselor. I clearly noticed a correlation between excessive access to screens at home and being quite active and dysregulated at school. Kids who spent a lot of time on screens at home had a hard time staying in the present moment and focusing their attention on the lessons at school.

I always had to start with the basics of understanding our senses and how they affect our internal state. Then as they grasped that concept, we would start to talk about feelings and identify where we felt feelings in our bodies. We were able to build on the learning of the senses to define our feelings and notice what those feelings needed.

Sometimes witnessing a feeling and experiencing it in our bodies is all that needs to happen for that energy to process and move through our bodies. Other times, those feelings are a bit stuck and have messages for us about what they need. I would guide kids through meditations and help them get into a state of mindfulness so they could tune in to themselves and observe all that was happening inside and outside of their bodies. As kids reach this level, they can then use this skill to check in with themselves throughout the day and track the mind-body connection that gives them clues about what they need from their environment or others.

—Kelly

When it comes to mindfulness for our children, there are two concepts we want to teach our children:

- The strategies to engage with curiosity in the present moment
- The ability to slow down and check in with one's mind and body

When we practice these concepts on a regular basis, the state of presence that we reach extends beyond core beliefs. We embody our most true and authentic experience of life. Being able to practice mindfulness is one of the best things we can do to support healthy core beliefs and remain intimately connected to our internal state.

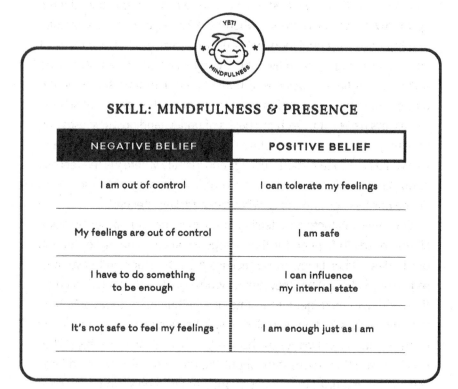

SKILL: MINDFULNESS & PRESENCE

NEGATIVE BELIEF	POSITIVE BELIEF
I am out of control	I can tolerate my feelings
My feelings are out of control	I am safe
I have to do something to be enough	I can influence my internal state
It's not safe to feel my feelings	I am enough just as I am

When I had my first son, I remember looking in his eyes in the hospital before we left to bring him home, and just bursting into tears. He was so beautiful, innocent, and so fully present and connected to me. He had literally been inside of me for nine months, and all of a sudden I was gazing into his eyes. I remember how that moment sucked me in. I felt an intensity of emotion that I had not had access to or even remembered feeling until that moment. Of course that moment was fleeting, and when we got home, we were in the throes of figuring out how to be first-time parents. But in connecting with my baby, I had an invitation to take respite from all the worry, learning, and buzz all around. I had a pathway to feeling fully present with him. I could join him and find quiet, and as he grew, I could help him understand how to get back this place of calm and connection as his mind started to form.

—Kelly

AFFIRMATION

With my heart open
and my mind open too,
I explore the world,
I am present with you.

USING MINDFULNESS FOR STRESS/ANXIETY

There has been much research over the years that suggests mindfulness practices can be particularly beneficial for children who exhibit signs of stress, anxiety, or emotional overwhelm. These signs might include frequent mood swings, trouble focusing, difficulty sleeping, or overreacting to minor problems. It's important to teach kids how to tune in and check in with themselves.

While kids are learning the skills of emotion identification and emotional fluency, mindfulness can teach them to check in with themselves in a variety of ways. Our bodies store emotions and energy and often show it before we can even explain it.

SUPPORTING OVERSTIMULATION AND DYSREGULATION

Have you ever felt anxiety in your body? Have you felt that racing, restless feeling that just kind of nags at you and consumes your inner world? Maybe you bite your lip, pick at your fingernails, or fidget as a tell when you're feeling that way. Many of us adults who experience anxiety know when it's there, and we have our go-to strategies like taking a walk, doing a meditation, or taking a deep breath.

Kids feel those same things—and they can be taught to recognize them early so they can find ways to regulate. Don't you wish we had this insight into our bodies and internal worlds when we were growing up?

The following is an example of how we help pre-K and school-age children start to self-identify when their body and mind might benefit from some mindfulness strategies to stay in the "ready-to-learn," calm state.

Kids need to know that sometimes our insides can feel fast or slow, even when we are sitting still. Our heart can beat fast in our chest, or our body can feel slow and droopy. When our bodies are feeling like they're moving too fast or too slow, there are tools we can use at school and at home to help our bodies feel just right.

TOO SLOW	JUST RIGHT	TOO FAST
Sometimes our bodies are feeling like they're moving too slow.	**Sometimes our bodies are feeling like they're moving and feeling just right.**	**Sometimes our bodies are feeling like they're moving too fast.**
Show kids what a "Too Slow" feeling might look like in the body:	**Sometimes people say this is a calm feeling.**	Show kids what a "Too Fast" feeling might look like in the body:
• Shoulders slumped	Show kids what a "Just Right" feeling might look like in the body:	• Jumping up and down
• Arms draped by your side (when standing)	• Sitting or standing up tall	• Pacing around
• Head resting on your hands (when seated)	• Smile or calm look on your face	• Tapping a pencil on the table
• Head lying on the table	• Hands resting in your lap or on the table (when seated)	• Moving your feet quickly under the desk
		• Moving around in your chair

MAKE A REGULATION TOOLBOX

Using items you have in your home, create a toolbox with your child. This toolbox can be used when they need to calm down, or when they're feeling slow and their body needs to gain energy. Let your child decide what works best for them. What is a tool that energizes them, and what tools help them feel calmer?

REGULATION TOOL SUGGESTIONS:

Deep Breathing

Hugs

Weighted Blankets

Reading a Book

Playing with Play-Doh or Kinetic Sand

Music

Looking at a Family Picture

Sensory Bottle/Calming Jar (Recipe Below)

Balance Board

Walk/Exercise/Yoga

BUILD YOUR OWN SENSORY BOTTLE

for children and grown-ups to create together

SUPPLIES:

Plastic Water Bottle
Water
Food Coloring
Baby Oil
Glitter (optional)

DIRECTIONS:

Remove the label from the water bottle.

Fill the water bottle half full with baby oil.

Add glitter if you desire.

Fill the remainder of the bottle with water, leaving
a small amount of space at the top.

Add 3-8 drops of food coloring of your choice.

Place the lid back on the water bottle.
We recommend gluing the lid on the bottle.

Shake your Sensory Bottle and watch the
color and glitter swirl.

AFFIRMATION

I slow down and am calm.
I sit very still.
I take deep breaths,
relax and chill.

PARENT REFLECTION MOMENT: MINDFULNESS

Now that you've learned a little about mindfulness, let's explore your own relationship with these moments of presence and checking in. Some people find these moments peaceful and replenishing, while others, especially if new to the practice, can find mindfulness a bit stressful or disorienting at first. This doesn't mean you are doing it wrong—it's just something to practice. Here are some questions to consider if you would like to implement our CALM Moment with a focus on Mindfulness. You can return to Chapter 5, pages 98–100 ("CALM Moments") to have an outline of this process as you engage in the following Reflection Questions:

- What is being triggered within me right now? Is this related to my feelings of adequacy as a parent? Am I feeling overwhelmed or overstimulated in some way?

- What does my body need at this moment for comfort and ease?

  For ongoing mindfulness practice, ask yourself:

- What are my preferred methods of practicing mindfulness? Is it through lighting a candle, meditation, yoga, walking, or spending time outdoors?

- What kinds of reminders or practices would assist me in becoming more present with myself and with my family?

Things to Remember

- Mindfulness for kids and caregivers can reduce stress, increase focus, and regulate emotions.
- To engage in mindfulness, you need to slow down and be present.
- Checking in with your sensory input can help you get into a mindful state.
- There are a number of regulation tools you can use with your kids, including music, reading, and hugs.

SLUMBERKINS CHARACTER CONNECTION: YETI

CHAPTER 9

Emotional Courage

All Feelings Welcome is more than the title of this book; it is at the heart of the whole approach. Many of us grew up when all feelings were *not* welcome, and we needed to hide away feelings that were seen as negative, like mad, sad, disappointed, embarrassed, and so on. Pushing our feelings aside or bottling them up actually reinforces the patterns that bring these uncomfortable feelings back to the surface of our awareness over and over again. We may struggle to understand why we keep ending up having the same difficult experiences in our relationships and lives again and again. We might attribute it to other people, situations, or just bad luck.

We believe it is in our power to shift these experiences from the inside out. When we welcome *all* our feelings, seeing them as friends and messengers giving us information about our needs, we build the foundation of emotional courage. When we cultivate the courage to embrace all the feelings and parts of ourselves, we are able to give that same courage and compassion to others as we navigate the world. This is where mindfulness can be so useful to us as a skill that helps us identify emotions. (For more on mindfulness, read the previous chapter.) Once we know which feelings are coming up, we can take a closer look at each feeling and get curious about the underlying need.

For example, if we're feeling mad, it can mean something didn't go the way we had planned. If we're feeling sad, it tells us that we care about something enough to cry. If we're feeling scared, we might need to make sure we are safe. Even looking at the feelings associated with more positive mindsets like happiness are clues that we are in a good place. Once we embrace the concept of welcoming feelings with curiosity and trying to understand what they're trying to tell us, they don't feel so scary anymore.

EMBRACING EMOTIONAL COURAGE

Emotional courage refers to the capacity to embrace and express your emotions fully, even when it may be challenging or uncomfortable to do so. When you have emotional courage, you can acknowledge and value all feelings, regardless of whether they are perceived as positive or negative.

Emotional courage is rooted in the idea that all emotions are valid and integral to personal growth and understanding.

There are many benefits to embracing emotional courage, and we were inspired to highlight this skill as we (along with the rest of the world, seemingly) came to understand the importance of vulnerability. Brené Brown has been a champion at helping shift cultural awareness about the meaning of vulnerability when she defined it in her book, *Braving the Wilderness*, as:

> The definition of vulnerability is uncertainty, risk, and emotional exposure. But vulnerability is not weakness; it's our most accurate measure of courage. When the barrier is our belief about vulnerability, the question becomes: "Are we willing to show up and be seen when we can't control the outcome?" When the barrier to vulnerability is about safety, the question becomes: "Are we willing to create courageous spaces so we can be fully seen?"

We want to help shift the narrative that being strong means being "controlling, hiding, or having no emotions." We want kids to have a framework to learn about all of their emotions early on so the concept of emotional courage, feelings, and sensitivity will not point to weakness but rather to great strength, leadership skills, and courage.

We now know that old beliefs like the following have been working against us in our own systems:

- "Boys don't cry."
- "Put on a happy face."
- "Grin and bear it."

We want to help kids embrace *all* their emotions.

My son Owen is the epitome of an athlete in the making. He's a sports-loving kid who wants to play basketball, football, and baseball year-round. As much as I've fought against the traditional narratives like "Big kids don't cry" at home, he's definitely heard them—from coaches, from friends, and from some of his own family.

Owen is also a deeply sensitive, deeply feeling kid. He likes to claim that if he was a character in the Slumberkins world, he is a mix of Fox and Ibex. I have taken a very proactive approach to try to instill the belief that all feelings are welcome, that being vulnerable is actually a strength, and that there are ways to feel emotions that actually empower us. He's had to *learn* how to be in touch with his mad or sad (not that mad or sad aren't welcome).

I had a moment where I saw a lot of the proactive work pay off the other night when we were reading *Ibex Feels Deeply*, one of the books in our Emotional Courage collection from Slumberkins. It reads: "Where is a place that you can go to feel at peace and let feelings show?" and his immediate answer was (cue the happy tears!) "I go to you, Mama."

In that moment, I knew that I was doing my job of being an emotional safe space for him through navigating all of the feelings that have come his way. I can't and won't fix them, but I can be there as a support and allow space for them to be said and acknowledged. I know that he can come to me to talk about anything upsetting that he might hear on the field, on the court, or at school.

Don't get me wrong, we have not perfected emotional processing or regulating. We still make mistakes when I try to rush the process. But I've learned that consistency is key. The most important thing to me as a mom is that he knows and understands that feeling all of his feelings is actually a superpower and will help him become a leader in whatever he chooses to do someday.

—Callie

When it comes to building emotional courage in our children, there are two concepts we want to teach our children:

- Being able to welcome emotions with curiosity
- Understanding that sensitivity (or feeling our feelings) is a strength

For emotional courage, the core belief that is being built is the concept of vulnerability and lovability.

SKILL: EMOTIONAL COURAGE

NEGATIVE BELIEF	POSITIVE BELIEF
I cannot feel mad or sad	My feelings are welcome
I have to hide my feelings	Having feelings is a strength
How I feel doesn't matter	My feelings matter
Being sensitive is bad	Sensitivity is a strength
I have to ignore my own needs	It's OK to take care of my own needs

PROACTIVELY BUILDING EMOTIONAL COURAGE

The kind of courage we want our future generation to embrace is not one of fake toughness, posturing, or making empty statements about greatness. It's the kind of courage that is soft and strong at the same time. It's the kind that opens our hearts instead of shutting them. Emotional courage is something we carry deep within us that helps us notice and embrace our tougher feelings. It's about finding resilience through hard things and embracing tough conversations. It's important for our children to know that we can be tough, open, and loving, all at the same time. For many of us, it's a new type of courage to learn about. It is a courage that we grow from deep inside, one that we can practice and develop.

We believe that if children learn emotional courage from a young age, they will carry this learning into any role they take on as an adult. We all can benefit from exploring how to show up and do the right thing, even when it's hard.

The ability to access emotional courage is such a supportive skill to offer a child for their life journey. When thinking about our own struggles that we have felt and seen, we believe emotional courage will empower children to handle a variety of difficult situations, many of which were not necessarily often outwardly discussed with us as children. Things like:

- Tolerating distressing and uncomfortable feelings (like sadness and guilt) without the need to avoid, numb feelings, or blame others
- Regulating emotions and learning from emotional states
- Asking for help when needed
- Feeling OK with not having all the answers
- Having conversations that may be uncomfortable but necessary
- Standing up for what you know is right

MODELING EMOTIONAL COURAGE

Emotional courage is not one of those things that we can just "tell" our children about; we have to show it. The way we relate to emotions, the things we value and don't value, the things we respond to and don't respond to are oftentimes unspoken "rules" in a family that everyone understands on some level, including children. This is why parents must be the ones to do the work first to make sure that children can learn from us as models of the behaviors and qualities we hope to grow in our children.

Here are some tips to help you get started if you are interested in building emotional courage in your family:

Notice your feelings: If we can face our own feelings, even the really strong ones, then you can do anything!

Accept all your feelings: We cannot move through a place of courage and bravery without acknowledging what is challenging us. Only once we accept what is can we move through it to a new place.

Let go of perfection: We all have challenges, we all make mistakes, and we all have big feelings. When we let go of being "perfect," it allows us to notice how things really are and shows us what we need to do from here.

Listen to others: Sometimes we get caught in our own heads and our own feelings, but if we take a moment to peek out with curiosity, we can learn from others and access information that can be really helpful to us.

Building emotional courage means coming back to core beliefs about being able to handle and hold all emotions by understanding that our emotions are messengers for our deeper needs. Emotional courage is not a destination; it's a journey. It's a constant process we can engage in to listen deeply to ourselves and others, and it's a conscious choice to value empathy and love over toughness and power.

AFFIRMATION

I feel very deeply.
I'm brave and I'm strong.
When I welcome my feelings,
I can never go wrong.

SUPPORTING A HIGHLY SENSITIVE OR DEEPLY FEELING CHILD

We want to make sure you know before reading any further that we see sensitivity as a superpower and an essential leadership skill. Even so, a parent who is a highly sensitive person (HSP), a child who is an HSP, or the parent of a child who is an HSP can face a long, confusing road to identifying and understanding this superpower. Dr. Elaine Aron pioneered research in the area of HSPs, and there has since been much added.

Identifying a highly sensitive child involves noticing certain key traits. These children often exhibit deep emotional reactions to both positive and negative experiences and may become easily overwhelmed by sensory stimuli like loud noises, bright lights, or strong smells. They tend to be highly empathetic and may react intensely to the emotions of others; they may also become upset by distressing scenes in movies or books. Highly sensitive children often require more time to make decisions, reflecting their deep processing of information and contemplation of outcomes. They might also have a rich inner life, displaying creativity and imagination but may be more prone to anxiety or shyness, especially in new or busy environments. These children usually seek comfort in familiar routines and may react strongly to changes or surprises. Recognizing these signs can help in providing the right support and environment to nurture their unique qualities.

It's important to remember that being highly sensitive is a normal trait, and these signs are part of how an HSP interacts with the world. Understanding and accommodating these sensitivities can help HSPs manage their environment more effectively.

If you suspect your child is a highly sensitive person, understanding and supportive approaches can be immensely beneficial for their development and well-being. Here are steps you can take:

Educate yourself about HSPs: Learn as much as you can about the trait of high sensitivity. Books, articles, and resources by Aron are particularly helpful.

Create a supportive environment: Create a calm, predictable home environment and be mindful of overstimulation from loud noises, bright lights, or chaotic situations.

Validate their feelings: Avoid phrases like "Don't be so sensitive" or "You need to toughen up," which can be dismissive and damaging.

Teach coping strategies: Help your child develop strategies to manage overstimulation and intense emotions. This can include teaching them calming techniques like deep breathing, finding a quiet space to decompress, or using sensory tools like noise-canceling headphones in loud environments.

Encourage open communication: Foster an environment in which your child feels comfortable discussing their feelings and experiences. Regular check-ins where they can talk about what's working for them—and what's not—can be very helpful.

Focus on their strengths: Highly sensitive children often have great empathy, creativity, and intuition. Encourage and nurture these strengths.

Set realistic expectations: Understand and communicate that it's OK to step back from overwhelming situations. Teach them it's fine to express their needs, such as needing a break during high-stress situations.

Seek professional guidance if needed: If your child is struggling, consider consulting with a psychologist or counselor who has experience with highly sensitive children.

Educate others: Inform key people in your child's life (like teachers and family members) about the trait of high sensitivity so they can also provide understanding and support.

AFFIRMATION

I feel very deeply,
it's a powerful gift.
There is strength inside me,
to guide and uplift.

PARENT REFLECTION MOMENT: EMOTIONAL COURAGE

It's not easy to face our own feelings, or address tough conversations or conflicts that need our attention. If you find yourself in a moment that calls for Emotional Courage. Here are some questions to consider if you would like to implement our CALM Moment with a focus on Emotional Courage. You can return to Chapter 5, pages 98–100 ("CALM Moments") to have an outline of this process as you engage in the following Reflection Questions.

In moments of struggle, when seeking clarity and self-comfort, ponder these questions:

- What is my immediate need or boundary right now?
- What am I avoiding, or what fears are present in this situation?
- How can I proceed with internal confidence and bravery?

For a broader reflection on emotional resilience:

- Are there specific emotions I usually avoid? What were my learnings about these emotions in childhood? Was it safe to express them?
- What lessons do I want to teach my child/children about emotions and vulnerability? How can I embody these teachings?

Things to Remember

- Emotional courage refers to the capacity to embrace and express your emotions fully.
- It's important for your children to know that you can be tough, open, and loving, all at the same time.
- The best way to teach children about emotional courage is to model it yourself.
- Being a highly sensitive person makes certain aspects of life more challenging, but reframing it as a gift empowers kids to see it as a leadership quality.

SLUMBERKINS CHARACTER CONNECTION: IBEX

CHAPTER 10

Gratitude

Perhaps you've just served dinner and your preschooler comes to the table, wrinkles up her nose, and says emphatically, "I'm not eating that." Or perhaps it's your toddler's birthday party, and they are ripping off wrapping paper left and right, but they don't even stop to thank the gift-giver. The moments when our children don't show gratitude can be very triggering for us. We might begin to worry that they don't appreciate what they have and start to wonder. . .will they be like this forever?

Many of us want our children to experience and practice gratitude, but how can we teach gratitude? Is learning to say thank you enough?

According to experts, gratitude is more than just saying thank you. It's an emotion that people can experience or express that requires a complex set of social-emotional skills. To feel grateful, we must be able to notice that something feels positive and then be able to attribute the "positive outcome" to something or someone outside of ourselves. In other words, children need to be able to notice their own emotions; identify the actions, feelings, or motivations of someone else; and then reflect on the impact that person has on them.

These are all complex skills that children often do not begin to utilize until they are three to five years old. But we don't have to wait until their third birthday to start teaching gratitude. We can start supporting foundational development from day one.

EMBRACING GRATITUDE

Gratitude isn't just a buzzword. Thinking about the good things in our lives actually affects the brain in several stress-busting, happiness-boosting ways. According to studies, feelings of gratitude have been shown to increase levels of neurotransmitters related to happiness (dopamine and serotonin), calm activity in the part of the brain associated with negative emotions, and reduce levels of cortisol (the stress hormone).

Expressing gratitude is a proactive, positive life skill that is truly a practice. You're not trying to solve a problem; you're trying to teach yourself something new. By practicing our sense of gratitude, it gets healthier and stronger. Over time, it becomes second nature to have a more positive point of view.

Mindfulness and gratitude go hand in hand. We believe that both practices supercharge your ability to stay in balance, no matter what's going on, and be in alignment with feelings of calm and connection to self and others. (You can read more in Chapter 8, "Mindfulness.")

When I worked as the school counselor, I had the opportunity to teach classes and try to give all students access to emotional learning skills that would benefit them in their day-to-day lives. One of my favorite memories was creating a kindness project with my first-grade students. It was meant to be a meaningful project that the whole class could do to make an impact in their school community. I had been interested in the research I had read about gratitude practices and wondered if it would be beneficial to integrate a brief gratitude practice to kick off our lessons. So before we dove into our kindness project, I introduced the students to a simple yet profound practice of gratitude.

Each day, we would start our time together with our gratitude practice. The students, initially hesitant, soon embraced this ritual with enthusiasm. We would share about the people in their lives who made them feel loved, the joy they found in their favorite foods, the excitement of playtime, and even the comfort they derived from their pets. This practice helped them identify the many ways that gratitude showed up in their lives. They went from thinking gratitude meant "saying thank you" to recognizing and appreciating the abundance in their everyday lives.

One particular instance stood out. A shy boy, often reserved and on the periphery of classroom activities, spoke about his gratitude for his grandmother's stories. This opened a floodgate of shared experiences among the students, revealing common ground that had previously been unnoticed. The practice of expressing gratitude began to bring the class together in new ways.

As the days passed, I felt the gratitude practice subtly shift the mood and behavior in the classroom. Students who once competed for attention began to listen and respond to each other with greater kindness and respect. They started to notice small acts of generosity and kindness that previously went unrecognized. These small moments of gratitude practice laid the foundation for a deeper understanding of kindness and compassion. It taught the students that kindness is not just an action but a state of being; it's a way to view the world and the people in it with a heart full of appreciation.

—Kelly

When it comes to building gratitude in our children, there are two concepts we want to teach our children:

- The ability to recognize what brings appreciation and love into their lives
- The understanding that we are surrounded by gifts in nature that aren't "things"

For gratitude, the core beliefs that are being built are often related to the concepts of abundance and scarcity.

SKILL: GRATITUDE, ABUNDANCE MINDSET & PRESENCE

NEGATIVE BELIEF	POSITIVE BELIEF
I don't have enough (Scarcity mindset)	I have what I need
There's a limited amount of good things in the world	I am lovable
I don't matter	I matter
I have to fight for good things to happen to me	There is not a limit on love (abundance vs. scarcity)
The more things I have, the better I am	There is endless (infinite) love available in the world
Things define me	My love grows, the more I give it

PROACTIVELY PROMOTING GRATITUDE

Cultivating gratitude in a child's life is profoundly beneficial as it lays the foundation for a positive and resilient mindset. When children learn to appreciate the good in their lives, they develop a sense of contentment and perspective that can buffer them against the inevitable challenges and disappointments they will face. Gratitude helps children look beyond themselves and understand their interconnectedness with others, fostering empathy and compassion.

Gratitude shifts children's focus from what they *lack* to what they *have*, promoting a mindset of abundance rather than scarcity. This outlook can significantly enhance their ability to embrace positive emotions; gratitude is closely linked with increased happiness, improved mental health, and stronger relationships. Additionally, when children practice gratitude, they tend to be more engaged in their communities, kinder, and more appreciative of diversity and the contributions of others. In essence, gratitude is not just a feeling but a practice that, when woven into the fabric of daily life, can profoundly shape a child's worldview, helping them grow into well-rounded, empathetic, and resilient adults.

The absence of gratitude in early childhood can significantly influence the development of core beliefs, shaping a child's outlook on life in profound ways. Without the practice of gratitude, children may develop a tendency to take things, people, and situations for granted, leading to a sense of entitlement or dissatisfaction. This lack of appreciation can foster a worldview centered on scarcity and lack, where the focus is more on what they *don't* have rather than on the abundance around them.

Such a mindset can lead to constant striving for more without recognizing or valuing current blessings, contributing to feelings of emptiness or unhappiness. Additionally, without gratitude, children might struggle to recognize and empathize with the efforts and feelings of others, impacting their ability to form deep and meaningful relationships. They may also have a diminished ability to find joy and contentment in simple pleasures, leading to a perpetual state of seeking external validation or material satisfaction. In essence, nurturing gratitude in early childhood is key to developing a sense of contentment, empathy, and a positive, balanced perspective on life.

SHIFTING AWAY FROM FOCUS ON MATERIAL POSSESSIONS

We all want our children to be grateful for all of the things life has to offer, and yet, we have all been the parent carrying them out of Target like a football because they can't get the thing they are currently fixated on, or we are embarrassed because they forget to say thank you when they receive a gift, or they tend to complain (loudly and often) that they don't have enough of what their friend has.

Shifting a child's focus from material possessions to a broader sense of gratitude is a gradual process that involves teaching and modeling appreciation for nonmaterial aspects of life.

AFFIRMATION

I have all that I need,
there are gifts all around.
I'm grateful in my heart
for the love I have found.

GRATITUDE AND NATURE

In today's world, our children are increasingly aware of global issues such as climate change, environmental degradation, and natural disasters. Because of this, the practice of gratitude can be a guiding light. Instilling a sense of gratitude in our young ones helps them develop a deeper appreciation and respect for nature and our planet. When children learn to be grateful for the earth and its resources, they begin to understand the intrinsic value of the natural world. Gratitude can anchor them in a positive mindset, enabling them to recognize the beauty and fragility of our environment. It fosters a sense of responsibility and stewardship, encouraging proactive attitudes toward conservation and sustainability.

Research indicates a connection between gratitude and appreciation for nature. This relationship is often explored within the context of positive psychology, which studies the factors that contribute to human happiness and well-being. Studies have shown that acknowledging the beauty and vastness of nature can lead to feelings of gratitude, due in part to the fact that nature often inspires awe. When individuals experience awe in natural settings, they are more likely to feel a deeper connection to something larger than themselves, which can cultivate gratitude.

Cultivating gratitude can be integrated into family outings in nature that can foster a deep appreciation for the natural world and its myriad of gifts. One effective approach is to spend regular time outdoors, helping your family members immerse themselves in nature's beauty and diversity.

This can include activities like hiking, gardening, or simply observing the changing seasons and wildlife in a local park. During these experiences, encourage mindful observation by paying close attention to the sights, sounds, and smells of nature and acknowledging the intricate details and interconnectedness of the natural environment.

You can also engage in conversations about how nature contributes to our well-being, such as providing food, clean air, and water, as well as being a source of beauty and inspiration. This can lead to discussions about the importance of environmental conservation and the role each person can play in protecting natural resources.

Additionally, participating in environmental stewardship activities, such as tree planting, community clean-ups, or wildlife conservation projects, can enhance a sense of gratitude and responsibility toward nature.

By combining these outdoor practices with reflection and gratitude exercises, such as writing about or sharing what one appreciates about nature, you can help your child develop a deeper, more meaningful connection with the natural world. This connection not only nurtures gratitude but also promotes a sense of peace and well-being, reinforcing the vital relationship between humans and the environment.

AFFIRMATION

I care for the Earth
and it cares for me.
We are all connected
and grateful to be.

PARENT REFLECTION MOMENT: GRATITUDE

Maybe you want to have a gratitude practice in your life, or maybe you have noticed that you are struggling with feeling you don't have "enough" of something in your life. Perhaps you are frustrated by your child asking for more and more, without noticing what they have. Here are some questions to consider if you would like to implement our CALM Moment with a focus on Gratitude. You can return to Chapter 5, pages 98–100 ("CALM Moments") to have an outline of this process as you engage in the following Reflection Questions.

In moments of struggle, when seeking clarity and self-comfort, ponder these questions:

- Is this situation bringing up any memories from my own past?
- Is this situation triggering any worries feelings of scarcity of resources or a deeper feelings around my capability or enough-ness?

For practicing gratitude more broadly, consider these prompts:

- What is something I feel grateful for today?
- What ways feel good for me to notice and appreciate nature and the world around me?

Things to Remember

- Gratitude is more than just saying thank you.
- Mindfulness, gratitude, and nature are all interconnected.
- Gratitude shifts children's focus from what they *lack* to what they *have*.

SLUMBERKINS CHARACTER CONNECTION: HONEY BEAR

CHAPTER 11

Self-Esteem

We throw the term *self-esteem* around in everyday conversation so often that it tends to lose its therapeutic meaning. We use it to describe someone who seems to be outwardly succeeding ("Oh, she just got the lead in the play. Her self-esteem just skyrocketed!") or seemingly failing ("He just can't seem to stay out of detention. His self-esteem is in the toilet."). But what does it actually mean, and how can we cultivate a sense of positive self-esteem in our kids?

The early relationship between parent and child shores up the foundation of self-concept and self-esteem, which is a sense of confidence in one's own abilities. Parents are the best first teachers of our children's emotional health; they are essential to the way in which they will grow to regard themselves. It is much easier to proactively build their confidence and self-esteem while they are still spending the majority of their hours in your care.

A child will suffer some blows to their self-esteem once they start spending time away from you. After all, we're guessing you can probably recall at least one specific insult another child hurled at you in your early years; the aggressor likely didn't lose sleep over the insult, but you might have. If a child hears those negative messages on repeat, it's not surprising that negative core beliefs start to form. Once their innate self-worth and lovability have taken a hit, it can be difficult to bounce back from that on their own.

NURTURING SELF-ESTEEM IN CHILDREN

When we worked as educators in the schools, we engaged with students who had very low self-esteem; they were often labeled the "bad kids" after years of behavioral issues or emotional outbursts in classrooms. We were ultimately called upon to support them to get them back on track. We know firsthand how difficult it is to build up a child's self-esteem after it's been challenged, especially if children have begun to form negative core beliefs. A child with low self-esteem is never a lost cause, however. We know this through our work with caseloads of students labeled as the "bad kids" over the years. We supported their emotional health and built their self-esteem by providing them with small wins, positive experiences, and affirmations. These gave them the opportunity to gain confidence in themselves. Brick by brick, they slowly built up their self-esteem.

Every child is going to have their feelings hurt at some point. Every child will feel out of place. Every child will feel like they are different in some way that impacts their self-esteem. We cannot control the amount or degree of adversity they will face. Their self-esteem will be challenged at many points down the line. But the foundation that you laid will be their bedrock, their strong base of support. When they are wrestling with their emotions and questioning their worth or lovability, they can lean back on the positive core beliefs that you have already started to help them form.

When I was in the fifth grade, I was the tallest kid in my class by at least a foot. One day, my "best friend" made fun of me in front of many of our classmates for being so tall. I wanted to disappear. I was mostly embarrassed, but I was also devastated, sad, and confused that the insult had come from my best friend.

I went home and told my mom what had happened, sobbing and complaining about being so tall. My mom immediately reminded me of all the positives that being tall afforded me and said that it was a unique quality that I would love someday. In that moment, my friend's words still stung. But I also remember feeling a sliver of hope that maybe my mom could be right.

She was intentionally shining light into my life and speaking words of positivity that I would latch on to for years, and even now as an adult.

The emotional foundation she had laid while providing experiences for me to gain confidence really did make a difference. Tall jokes may have made me cringe in the moment, but the scales had started to tip in the right direction of positive self-esteem and confidence.

When Kelly and I were developing the Bigfoot character for Slumberkins, all of this experience played a role in the book *Bigfoot Copes with Hurt Feelings*. We purposefully created books that encourage children to go the extra mile and repeat positive affirmations out loud at the end of the story. Even if a parent doesn't know the benefit of affirmations, we do, and that's why we're giving parents a shortcut, a done-for-you way to make an impact.

Reading the story and reciting affirmations on a nightly basis with my own children (who will likely grow taller than me someday) continues to bring so much healing for me as an adult, and at the same time, I am helping set them up for success in their own lives.

Recently, my son Owen was teased for being too tall to be a first grader, and was actually shoved to the ground. I immediately returned to the pain I had experienced as a child, and I began worrying about how this could impact my son's self-esteem.

But he seemed completely fine. He said, "I don't know why he shoved me. Being tall is a good thing, and I like being tall." He saw the incident for what it was; it wasn't about him. He didn't let it affect his self-concept.

It was such a healing moment for me as a parent to know that I am supporting my kids in the emotional realm and giving them that solid foundation that will set them up for success throughout their lives.

—Callie

TEACHING CHILDREN THEY ARE LOVED—AND LOVABLE

As much as we all want to protect our children from anything harmful that comes their way, it's an impossible task. The best thing we can do is to help them remember who they are, remember why they're special, and remember that they are loved—and lovable.

Keep in mind that there's a difference between the feeling of being loved and believing that you are innately lovable. Knowing you're lovable means that you know it's easy to love you and your innate qualities make you worthy of love. Being loved is knowing that there are people who care deeply about you. Self-esteem is built on the foundation of believing you are lovable.

When it comes to building a child's self-esteem, there are two concepts and skills we want to teach our children:

- As they grow, they will always be loved and have people who care about them.
- They need to be able to recognize their inner worth when facing challenges.

For self-esteem, the core belief that is being built is the concept of lovability.

SKILL: SELF-ESTEEM & CONFIDENCE

NEGATIVE BELIEF	POSITIVE BELIEF
I am unlovable	I am lovable
I don't like me (I am dumb, I am ugly, I am...)	I like me
People don't care about me	I have people who care about me
Others' opinions define me	I can decide how I feel about myself
I can't handle hard things	I can handle adversity

PROACTIVELY BUILDING POSITIVE BELIEFS

Building a child's self-esteem can seem like a tremendous responsibility—after all, we just spent several pages describing how important it is. It can feel overwhelming for that responsibility to rest solely on your shoulders. Don't worry, it's not all on you. Outside people and interactions will inevitably impact your child's self-esteem, but you can help shape how those interactions will be received with this proactive support. The path to positive self-esteem is surprisingly straightforward. You can start instilling this belief even before your child is able to walk or talk.

Self-esteem refers to a person's beliefs about their own value and worth. In early childhood, having positive self-esteem is critical as children begin to explore the world. We want to build their confidence in order to support them in exploring new things.

Not only does it shape what decisions they make, the types of activities they try, and how they respond to setbacks. It also builds their confidence to try new things and make good decisions, and overall helps them succeed in life.

Negative self-esteem is not considered a mental health diagnosis on its own, but is often a factor in anxiety and depression as well as relationship difficulties. On the other hand, when people feel positive about their worth, value, and innate lovability, they can navigate challenges in their environments, and feel happier and more fulfilled in their lives and relationships.

The deep beliefs we hold about ourselves and our worth often begin in early childhood. Anyone who has been to therapy as an adult understands that our negative beliefs are much harder to change once we grow up. This is why helping our children develop positive beliefs about themselves is so important from day one.

We can *tell* our children we love them and think they are great, but it's even better when we *show* them. When we provide a consistent environment that supports and values them, they will *feel* worthy and loved, and then will internalize this feeling as they grow.

I am so loved.
This will always be true.
As I grow and I learn,
I love myself too.

HELPING A CHILD WHO IS STRUGGLING WITH SELF-ESTEEM

Being on the receiving end of an insult isn't the only way a child's self-esteem can be damaged. They may also struggle with receiving criticism (especially from primary caregivers), comparing themselves with others, facing academic difficulty/pressure at school, lacking support or recognition, having unrealistic expectations placed upon them, and even hearing parents being critical of themselves or one another.

We are going to narrow in on hurt feelings and how to support your child through this emotional wound. You may find other blows to self-esteem covered in other chapters. For example, for unrealistic expectations placed on kids, please read Chapter 14, "Self-Acceptance."

If you know your child has had their feelings hurt, you can be their safe space. Let them process their emotions and accept any feelings they may have. Ask open-ended questions about any difficulties they're having.

Try to approach this conversation in a calm, nonjudgmental manner by:

Validating their feelings: Let your child know that their feelings matter and that they have a right to feel the way they do. This can help your child feel understood and supported and can encourage them to continue sharing their emotions with you. One of our favorite ways to validate someone's feelings is to say "Of course, it makes sense you are feeling this way."

Encouraging expression: Guide your child to express their emotions in a healthy and constructive way. If they're uncomfortable talking about how they're feeling, drawing can help.

Providing reassurance: Let your child know you are there to support them. Work with them to devise a plan to address the problematic situation, and let them know that you will be there every step of the way.

Establishing an affirmation practice: Use our examples or come up with an affirmation with your child that you both can easily remember and practice together daily.

TEACH KIDS HOW TO RESPOND

Once you've supported your child through the tough moment at hand, it's time to start (re)building their self-confidence and helping them to look forward in case a similar situation arises in the future. There isn't a one-size-fits-all method for how to do this, however. You and your child can work together to think of strategies that your child feels good about.

Find ways that your child can respond that feel comfortable for them and that they can carry out with confidence. Here are some examples:

Practice a confident posture: Teach your child to practice standing tall, with their shoulders and back strong and their hands unclenched. Take deep, regular breaths into the belly (which also helps with calming nerves).

Create a verbal response: Feelings of anger and embarrassment in the moment can leave your child feeling powerless and tongue-tied. Instead of trying to argue, call names, or yell, suggest that your child practice a brief, firm response, such as the following:

- "That's not funny."
- "I don't like it when you call me that."

- "That's not my name; please use my real name."
- "That was mean and really hurt my feelings."
- "What you're doing is not OK."
- "I'm not going to let your words affect me."
- "You're being hurtful. Stop it."

Walk away: Sometimes leaving a conflict is the strongest statement you can make. Let your child know there is nothing wrong with simply walking away and taking space from a situation without giving a response.

These types of responses can help your child take control of the situation and become a self-advocate in the moments when they've been hurt by others. And of course, always encourage them to talk to you about anything, especially if it's something that makes them feel hurt or uncomfortable. Just sharing their feelings can help the repair begin.

AFFIRMATION

I am kind. I am strong.
I am brave and unique.
The world is better because I am here.
I like me.

PARENT REFLECTION MOMENT: SELF-ESTEEM

If you catch yourself having your own big feelings while you observe your child's struggle with self-esteem, you might need to take a step back and heal yourself before healing your child. Here are some questions to consider if you would like to implement our CALM Moment with a focus on Self-esteem. You can return to Chapter 5, pages 98–100 ("CALM Moments") to have an outline of this process as you engage in the following Reflection Questions.

In moments of struggle, when seeking clarity and self-comfort, ponder these questions:

- Is this situation bringing up any memories from my own past?
- Is this situation triggering any worries about being good-enough as a parent?

If reflecting on self-esteem in general, try asking yourself. . . .

- Do I have someone in my life who offers me unconditional love? If so, how do they show it? If not, how can I show it to myself?
- What words of affirmation did I need to hear as a child? What affirmation can I say daily to support my own self-esteem?

Things to Remember

- You might want to rush in and "fix" your child's feelings, but that's not your job. They can't avoid hard feelings, and neither can you. But you can help them process those feelings.

- When children have strong core beliefs, they can return to them for support as those beliefs are challenged.

- Growth doesn't necessarily come from achievement; it comes from the process of holding space in the uncomfortable moments.

- As they gain experience and wisdom in working through hurt feelings, your child will be better prepared to handle future challenges to their self-esteem.

SLUMBERKINS CHARACTER CONNECTION: BIGFOOT

CHAPTER 12

Authenticity

"Authenticity is the daily practice of letting go of who we think we are supposed to be and embracing who we actually are."

—Brené Brown, *The Gifts of Imperfection*

To be authentic is to be true to yourself—to listen to the voice within. When we share our unique gifts, the whole world can benefit from what we have to offer. When we let our own light shine, we can attract meaningful friendships with people who appreciate us for who we are. Opening up to others brings us closer to people we care about—people who make us feel safe to play, create, and express ourselves in ways that make us feel good inside.

EXPLORING OUR AUTHENTIC SELVES

It's easy to think about our authentic selves as a version of ourselves that we must grow into over time. But learning how to recognize and trust your feelings, and to act in accordance with your values, is a process that begins in early childhood. As parents and caregivers, it's our job to help the little ones in our lives nurture the relationships they have with their inner voices. Teaching kids to live authentically can be challenging in a world that often seems to encourage conformity, but there are plenty of ways we can inspire young ones to embrace their authentic selves.

It's normal for us to want to identify with others and to pine for a sense of belonging among our peers. But sometimes this leads us to behave in ways that do not align with who we truly are. People often worry that if they let their own light shine, they will not be accepted by others. They fear that others will not understand them because they have a life experience and perspective that is different from their own. Showing our true selves to others is scary, but it is also an act of bravery. So just imagine how complicated this all must be for the young children in our lives, who are getting acquainted with their own thoughts, feelings, and preferences while also taking in and learning from the world around them. It's no surprise that children with strong models of authenticity in their lives are more likely to inhabit their own authentic identities.

There are huge ripple effects of authenticity for a child's life. Embracing authenticity in our lives and in our children's development brings a cascade of positive effects. Imagine a world where your child feels confident enough to express their true selves, where their creativity is not just a burst of color on a canvas but a reflection of their inner world. When our children are authentic, they form friendships not just based on common interests but on real, heartfelt connections. These are the friendships that weather life's storms. In being true to themselves, children learn to stand up for what they believe in, resist peer pressure, and grow in self-confidence. Think of authenticity as a garden where the unique gifts and talents of each child are celebrated and nurtured. Here, creativity isn't stifled but blooms in vibrant self-expression. This is the power of authenticity—it allows our children to shine in their true colors and shapes the world into a more inclusive, understanding place.

We asked our friend Krista to share her experience growing up in an environment where being different was difficult. She helps us shine a light on all of us as caregivers. Choosing not to actively talk about or celebrate differences and what makes each and every one of us unique can have lasting negative impacts on a child who doesn't feel like they belong.

I was in fifth grade and trying hard to belong, but just barely fitting in. I looked different than all my teachers and everyone in my class. Small things often reminded me I did not quite fit, like the color of the bandages available in the nurse's office, questions like "Where are you from?" or my teacher correcting my pronunciation of Samoa, where my family is from.

All of this set the background for our multicultural unit. Each student chose a random country and gave a presentation on that country. When it was my turn to present, my teacher told everyone that "Krista is actually from one of these countries." Kids then proceeded to comment on the ways I looked like people from the countries they studied. My teacher just sat there.

As I reflect on this experience, I have two takeaways. The first one is that what you do all year builds a foundation of moments that can create connection while celebrating all the ways we live our lives.

Additionally, use language that connects unique differences to our shared experiences. For example, instead of focusing on "those countries" in this project, we could have focused on family traditions. Family traditions would be different for all students and would center around the idea that we all have ways to feel connected to the people we love, which is often shown through tradition.

Ask yourself, "Am I doing everything I can to make the people in my life feel valued and included? What can I learn from people who have a different perspective, knowledge, or skill set than I do?"

At times, you may feel awkward or unsure of how to approach someone who is different than you in some ways, but when you lead with curiosity and genuine interest, you'll forge a more authentic connection and enrich your life in new and valuable ways.

—Krista Olson

When thinking about building authenticity into our children's lives, there are two skills we want our children to learn:

- Identifying and embracing their uniqueness in the world
- Finding the balance of staying true to self while navigating different environments and expectations

For authenticity, the core beliefs that are being built are the concepts of acceptance and safety.

SKILL: AUTHENTICITY

NEGATIVE BELIEF	POSITIVE BELIEF
I have to be a certain way to be accepted by others	I am wonderful just the way I am
I am unlovable	I am lovable
I don't belong	I belong
No one sees or loves me for who I am	I have people who love me for me
I have to hide who I am	I let my light shine
It's not OK to be different from others	It's OK to be myself

PARENTING TO PROACTIVELY FOSTER AUTHENTICITY

This intense desire to feel like we are part of a group is hardwired into our biology. Not long ago in human history, fitting in with the group impacted one's access to protection. Today, not "fitting in" with those in power can still be dangerous for marginalized groups.

That said, it's no surprise that kids go to great lengths to connect with those around them and seek a sense of belonging in groups. But there is a big difference between fitting in and true belonging.

"Fitting in" suggests kids don't feel comfortable being their authentic selves. For some children, "fitting in" may not even be a choice, as some qualities (appearance, for instance) are impossible to hide. Brené Brown defines "belonging," on the other hand, as "being part of something bigger but also having the courage to stand alone."

If you want to create an emotionally safe space for your child to *belong*, you must first look at your own feelings and internal reactions when they begin to express themselves.

For instance, if your oldest child is bossing your other kids or their friends around, use that as an opportunity to reflect. Do you feel annoyed? What did you learn about "bossy" behavior as a child? Were you allowed to be bossy as a child? What is another word for bossy? Can bossiness be a trait of a strong leader? All of these reflections can lead us to more insight and offer a way to reduce our own reactivity as we learn to show up for all children.

Once we have worked through our own biases and reactions, we can better show up for children and welcome all feelings. An *All Feelings Welcome* approach prioritizes the adult-child connection, which creates a sturdy foundation to experience true belonging.

Remember that it can be scary and overwhelming for children to express big feelings. When there is a foundation of emotional safety already established, children learn that they can share how they really feel inside and still be accepted. These early interactions help reinforce the permission to practice emotional courage as they venture into the world. As they grow, we hope they'll never forget that belonging comes from inside.

AFFIRMATION

I have my own magic,
my own inner light.
When I am true to myself,
it shines strong and bright.

BUILDING AUTHENTICITY WHEN YOU SENSE TROUBLE

When a child struggles to embrace authenticity, it can manifest in various ways that warrant attention. You may notice your child conforming excessively to peer or adult expectations, showing reluctance to express their true interests or feelings, or consistently suppressing their individuality to fit in. This might be accompanied by signs of low self-esteem, such as frequently comparing themselves negatively to others, or a lack of confidence in their own ideas and abilities. Additionally, children who struggle with authenticity may exhibit anxiety or discomfort in situations where they are encouraged to express themselves or make independent choices. It's important to observe these behaviors within the context of your child's overall development, as they can be indicators of underlying challenges in embracing their true self.

As parents, watching our children express themselves in ways that don't quite align with societal norms can stir a complex mix of emotions. It's natural to feel a twinge of worry or concern, not because we want to stifle their individuality, but because we wish to shield them from potential hurt, ridicule, or difficulties that might arise from being perceived as different. This protective instinct often stems from our own experiences; many of us have felt the sting of being judged or not fitting in at some point in our lives.

It's a delicate balance to acknowledge these fears while also championing our children's unique selves. We understand that trying to conform to societal expectations can be like wearing an ill-fitting garment—uncomfortable and constraining. Yet, we also know the harsh reality of a world that isn't always kind to those who stand out.

A starting point for any parent that may have these concerns or can see this behavior in their child would be to:

Encourage self-exploration: Create a safe and open environment where your child can explore and express their interests, feelings, and thoughts without fear of judgment. Engage in activities that allow them to discover and showcase their unique talents and preferences. This could be through art, music, writing, or any other medium that resonates with them. The key is to offer opportunities for self-expression and validate their choices and feelings.

Model authenticity: Children often learn by observing the adults around them. Show your child that it's OK to be yourself by being authentic in your own actions and communications. Share your thoughts and feelings openly, discuss your interests and hobbies, and demonstrate that it's OK to be different and to have unique opinions. By seeing authenticity in action, your child can learn to value and embrace their own individuality.

Positive reinforcement and validation: Recognize and celebrate your child's individual qualities and achievements, no matter how small. Provide positive reinforcement when they express themselves or make independent choices. Avoid comparing them to others and instead focus on their personal growth and unique attributes. Validation from a parent is powerful in reinforcing a child's sense of self-worth and encouraging them to continue expressing their true self.

Remember, each child is different, so it's important to be patient and attentive, adapting these approaches to fit your child's unique personality and circumstances.

UNDERSTANDING THE IMPACT OF SPIRITUAL AND CULTURAL BELIEFS

For parents who hold deeply rooted spiritual or cultural beliefs, imparting those to your children is natural and can be a profoundly rewarding aspect of parenting. However, it's essential to balance this with nurturing your child's authentic self-expression, even when it ventures into territories that might make you feel uneasy. The key lies in creating a space where family beliefs are shared with love and openness, rather than as unyielding directives.

Start by sharing your beliefs as part of family storytelling, making it clear that these are cherished values that guide your family's life. At the same time, encourage your child to explore, ask questions, and express their thoughts and feelings.

It's about letting kids know that while the family holds certain beliefs dear, their individual journey of understanding and expression is not only allowed but valued. The goal is not to mold your child's spiritual identity but to guide them lovingly, providing a foundation of family beliefs while nurturing their freedom to explore and express their authentic self.

AFFIRMATION

I am true to myself.
I let my light shine.
I can be who I am.
That's for me to define.

PARENT REFLECTION MOMENT: AUTHENTICITY

The topic of authenticity can bring up so many triggers for parents. Perhaps you worry that your child will not fit in with their peers, or maybe you are worried that they are dimming their own unique self to try to fit in with others. Either way, we as parents get caught up in worry and stress, not sure of how to help our kids move forward. If you are feeling triggered around this topic, it's important to check in with yourself. Here are some questions to consider if you would like to implement our CALM Moment with a focus on Authenticity. You can return to Chapter 5, pages 98–100 ("CALM Moments") to have an outline of this process as you engage in the following Reflection Questions.

In moments of struggle, when seeking clarity and self-comfort, ponder these questions:

- What emotions am I experiencing, and what might my child be feeling right now?
- What is my primary concern at this moment, and what does this worry require for resolution?

When contemplating Authenticity:

- Reflect on your own experiences with fitting in or standing out.
- Identify the people or places where you feel a true sense of belonging.
- Consider how you can foster a safe environment where your child can experience genuine belonging both with you and within your home.

Things to Remember

- To be authentic is to be true to oneself—to listen to the voice within.
- Though we value authenticity, keep in mind that not "fitting in" with those in power can still be dangerous for marginalized groups. We need to strike a balance.
- Tell your child that it's OK to think and feel differently, encouraging them to explore and express themselves freely.

SLUMBERKINS CHARACTER CONNECTION: UNICORN

Growth Mindset

As educators working with students who struggled in the school environment, we taught about the concept of "growth mindset" daily. Coined by psychologist Carol Dweck, a growth mindset is the belief that abilities and intelligence can be developed through dedication, hard work, and the right kind of encouragement. This is a contrast to a fixed mindset, where people believe their talents and abilities are innate gifts and unchangeable.

Oftentimes, our students had already had such low self-esteem and expectations of themselves that the concept of sticking with a challenging assignment often led to some pretty large emotional reactions or behavioral incidents. It was our job to reframe challenges as opportunities, model a new way of thinking, and instill a growth mindset that would be a foundation of how they approached all things in life. When you view something as a challenge to be solved rather than an obstacle standing in your way, your perspective shifts dramatically. The day can feel a little bit brighter, you feel more energized, and you can let go of the fear of failure.

CULTIVATING A GROWTH MINDSET

Dweck's research shows that encouragement plays a key role in shaping mindsets—in either direction. Complimenting a child's innate intelligence, for example, promotes a fixed mindset, whereas praising effort and perseverance develops a growth mindset. Studies have linked growth mindsets to greater academic achievement and emotional well-being. Kids who believe they can grow become more motivated learners, have a more positive attitude, and cope better with anxiety and adversity.

In other words, with thoughtfully crafted words of encouragement for kids, caregivers can teach growth mindset principles from an early age—setting them up for future success.

Fostering a growth mindset helps kids develop healthy self-esteem and self-compassion. Children learn to base their self-worth not on external markers of success or failure but on their own efforts and personal growth.

They learn to be kind to themselves during challenging times, understanding that struggle doesn't reflect on their worth as individuals.

As parents, we can nurture a growth mindset in our children through our language and actions. Praising effort rather than innate ability, encouraging persistence in the face of difficulty, and framing challenges as opportunities to learn and grow are all ways we can support this mindset. By doing so, we equip our children with a powerful foundation for emotional wellness, one that will serve them throughout their lives. This tool enables them to approach life with confidence, resilience, and a constant readiness to grow and adapt. In essence, cultivating a growth mindset is not just about preparing our children; it sets them up for a fulfilling, emotionally rich life. It's teaches them that their journey is not defined by the hurdles they encounter but by how they choose to navigate them. With a growth mindset, we're not just raising learners; we're nurturing future innovators, leaders, and emotionally well-rounded individuals.

> While we were developing Slumberkins into the brand you see today, we had some friends behind the scenes who would joke around with us that they couldn't believe that we just kept achieving what we were without having a strong idea of how it would all happen. No business plan to start, no degrees to give us credit to start a business. It always makes us laugh because from the outside, that definitely makes sense. I mean, we are two moms and educators who had absolutely no idea what we were doing when we started running a business.
>
> And that's actually the key to growth mindset right there. We were completely aware that we didn't know what we didn't know—and we weren't afraid to ask for help.
>
> For all of the shiny moments in building a business that you can see from the outside, there have been multiple "failures" and lessons learned along the way..and "success" all comes back to mindset.

Our mindset shifted to asking ourselves questions like: What can we learn from this experience? How can we grow from this? Who should we reach out to ask that question? How will we problem-solve for (insert a few hundred fires that needed to be put out)? Why not us? If not us, who will do this? How can the mission reach further than we originally thought?

We embraced the overwhelm of it all feeling too big, and put one foot in front of the other. We leaned on each other, mentors, partners, and our team of equally passionate moms who took the mission and goal of Slumberkins just as seriously as we did.

—Callie

When it comes to building a growth mindset in our children, there are two concepts we want to teach our children:

- The belief that setbacks can help us grow
- That they can try new things and always ask for help if they get stuck

For a growth mindset, the core beliefs that are being built are capability and cognitive flexibility.

SKILL: GROWTH MINDSET

NEGATIVE BELIEF	POSITIVE BELIEF
I can't do hard things	I can do hard things
Mistakes are bad	Mistakes help us grow
I have to do things on my own	I can ask for help
Asking for help is weak	Asking for help is OK
I can't try new things	I can try new things
I will fail	I am capable

PROACTIVELY BUILDING GROWTH MINDSET

Our words have immense potential to shape young minds. Verbal encouragement and positive reinforcement can help us build helpful thought patterns. Knowing how to talk to kids to encourage a positive mindset is important; phrases focused on effort and improvement help kids stay focused on sustainable motivation.

People are motivated in different ways, which are defined as either intrinsic or extrinsic.

- *Intrinsic* motivation comes from within—the inherent satisfaction of learning something new or overcoming a challenge.
- *Extrinsic* motivation is fueled purely by external rewards and praise, be that compliments or cookies.

The words we use when praising children impact their source of motivation. Compliments focused on effort, progress, and problem-solving promote intrinsic motivation. But conversations about speed, innate talent, and rewards shift motivation externally for a young child.

Studies show intrinsic motivation is more powerful for sustaining children's engagement and achievement in the long term. Keeping this in mind can help us craft encouragement that feeds an intrinsic growth mindset.

USING CONSTRUCTIVE WORDS OF ENCOURAGEMENT

The words caregivers use have a profound impact on growth mindset. Some of the most encouraging words for kids are those that validate their feelings while spotlighting their ability to learn and grow. In the following lists, you'll find 12 helpful phrases caregivers can use to cultivate growth mindsets across different scenarios.

Words That Reinforce Effort

Children benefit from knowing that *effort* fuels success—rather than innate talent. Using phrases that praise hard work over results teaches the power of perseverance. Here are some examples:

- "I see how focused you were drawing that picture. Your effort shows!"
- "I love how you kept trying different solutions until you solved that puzzle."

- "You put in so much practice—no wonder you're getting better at reading."
- "I know that assignment was tough, but you stuck with it. Great job not giving up!"

Emphasizing the learning process over grades or other subjective measures breeds motivation from within. Celebrate small wins that come from diligence and teamwork. Encourage revision over rushing to finish easy tasks quickly.

Words That Highlight Potential

Children benefit from feeling like they have the potential to grow and succeed. Here are encouraging words for kids in this scenario:

- "I believe in you. I know you can handle this challenge."
- "You're at the starting line of learning this. I'm excited to see your progress."
- "When something is hard, it just means your brain is growing!"
- "You might not know how yet—and that's OK. You'll figure it out, I'm sure of it."

Urge kids to embrace uncertainty as a path for growth, not something to fear. Try highlighting "yet" thinking, as in: "You can't do multiplication *yet*, but I know you'll get there with practice."

Words That Foster Curiosity and Learning

A child with a true growth mindset develops an innate love of learning through asking questions. Nurturing such natural curiosity is especially key for younger children. In this context, words of encouragement for kids should aim to celebrate their exploration, questions, and even mistakes. Here are some examples:

- "I love how curious you are about how things work."
- "Asking questions helps us learn. What else are you wondering about?"
- "Making mistakes just means you're learning. You'll do even better next time."
- "Look at how much you're learning by trying new things!"

Prompt children to come up with their own solutions before jumping in. Let them learn through hands-on exploration. Embrace mistakes as opportunities to improve. Above all, let your child lead—following their interests to fan the flames of curiosity.

Words to Avoid

Certain common phrases may promote a fixed mindset in children. Many of those phrases were things we were told in our childhood. Repeating them to our children feels natural, especially if they're complimentary but the language we use can subltly support or block our child's tendancies towards intrisic motivation vs. extrinsic.

Telling a young child "You are so smart!" implies that intelligence is innate. This could put pressure on them to live up to a label, undermining the value of effort. Similarly, praising good grades or easy wins instead of progress sends the message that success should just come naturally . . . and if it doesn't, there's no point in trying.

Other phrases may unintentionally minimize or dismiss a child's feelings. Saying "Don't worry" or "Shake it off" could convey that a child's emotions are unimportant. This shuts down opportunities for problem-solving big feelings together.

Children also might interpret dramatic praise like "Incredible job!" as meant for much bigger accomplishments. So using such phrases too freely can quickly dilute their positive impact.

Of course, there's nothing wrong with celebrating our kids' successes. However, focus your encouragement on the process *behind* the success to build resilience. Don't fret if you have a mixed bag in how you communicate these things to your child. Your intention to focus more on process will be felt more than saying the words exactly right all the time.

TAKING BREAKS AND WHY THEY ARE IMPORTANT

Taking a break is perhaps the most underrated of all the growth mindset concepts, but we think it's one of the most important. Resting, eating, and playing can help our kids feel refreshed and resilient. All living things need rest, including—or, especially!—our children. When we help our kids tune in to their bodies and minds and care for themselves, we are teaching them a key pillar of growth mindset that will support them and give them the energy to keep going.

One of the reasons we love the concept and practice of taking a break is that it teaches kids to tune in to the language of their bodies and minds. As parents, we can show them how to read their own cues so that later they can begin to do it themselves. When we see the need for a break arising, we can narrate this for them.

AFFIRMATION

I can do hard things.
I can pause or push through.
I trust my body and heart.
I know what to do.

HELPING SHIFT A FIXED MINDSET

As parents, we might spot signs of a fixed mindset in our little ones when they shy away from challenges, fearing failure or making mistakes. If your child often says things like "I can't do this; it's too hard" or "I'm just not good at this," it could be a hint that they're stuck in a fixed mindset. Another red flag is when they get easily frustrated, especially in the face of new tasks, or if they seem overly focused on proving themselves rather than learning and growing. Recognizing these signs is the first step in gently guiding them toward embracing a growth mindset. Remember, every child has the potential to develop a growth mindset, and it's our nurturing support that can guide them on this journey.

It's important to remember that mindsets are not set in stone; they can evolve and change over time. Start by creating an environment where mistakes and challenges are viewed as opportunities for learning and growth, rather than as failures. Emphasize the value of effort and perseverance over innate talent or immediate success. Praise their hard work, strategies, and determination, and share stories of people who achieved their goals through persistence and learning from setbacks.

Work with your child to set achievable, effort-based goals, and celebrate the small steps they take toward these goals. This reinforces the concept that growth and learning are gradual processes. You can then introduce them to activities that are slightly challenging but achievable, providing support and encouragement along the way. This will help build their confidence and resilience.

Open conversations about their feelings of defeat or reluctance to try new things are also crucial. Listen empathetically, validate their emotions, and help them reframe these experiences from a growth perspective.

TEACHING KIDS HOW TO RESPOND

Here are five actionable tips to gently guide a child from a fixed mindset to a more open, growth-oriented mindset:

Celebrate effort, not just success: Emphasize the value of effort and perseverance.

Use encouraging language: Swap out absolute phrases like "I can't do this" with "I can't do this yet."

Introduce role models: Share stories of people (real or fictional) who have overcome challenges through persistence.

Encourage curiosity and new experiences: Foster an environment where trying new things is celebrated, even if they don't go perfectly.

Problem-solve together: When your child faces a challenge, instead of solving it for them, work through it together.

Remember, the goal is to create a safe and supportive environment where your child feels comfortable taking risks, making mistakes, and learning from them.

AFFIRMATION

If I see a problem, I can fix it.
I can try to figure it out.
If I don't know what to do,
I can always ask for help.

PARENT REFLECTION MOMENT: GROWTH MINDSET

Parenting can be so overwhelming, and it's not always easy to see the path forward. It can also be so difficult to see our children struggling with giving up and sticking with hard things. Reflect on your own mindset before you work on your child's. Here are some questions to consider if you would like to implement our CALM Moment with a focus on Growth Mindset. You can return to Chapter 5, pages 98–100 ("CALM Moments") to have an outline of this process as you engage in the following Reflection Questions.

In moments of struggle, when seeking clarity and self-comfort, ponder these questions:

- Consider the beliefs that might be hindering your problem-solving ability. How can you view this situation from a different perspective?
- Assess whether the situation at hand is something you need help with, or if it's a challenge you can empower yourself to handle.
- When your child is facing difficulties, think about how to both validate their emotions and encourage their resilience and confidence to progress.

For general contemplation on fostering a growth mindset:

- Reflect on the balance you wish to achieve with your child in terms of knowing when to persevere and when to rest.
- Consider ways you can exemplify positive coping mechanisms in the face of challenges, demonstrating both perseverance and the wisdom to seek help when needed.

Things to Remember

- Growth mindset, the belief that you can develop your abilities through hard work and positive affirmations, often leads to academic achievement, resilience, and overall well-being.

- Children benefit from knowing that effort fuels success—rather than innate talent. The words we use can reinforce that belief.

- Allowing yourself to rest is just as important as learning and growing.

SLUMBERKINS CHARACTER CONNECTION: NARWHAL

CHAPTER 14

Self-Acceptance

Raise your hand if you've ever felt overwhelmed by "mom guilt" when you forgot to pack your child a school snack or because your home doesn't resemble those pristine images on Pinterest and Instagram. Or perhaps you envisioned a journey of breastfeeding, only to find stress dominating your postpartum days, leading to a decrease in milk supply, and now you're sitting there, harshly judging yourself. Maybe you love your job, yet you struggle with finding the balance at times, your child doesn't get the best version of you, and you beat yourself up over it. We completely get it. We've been there.

As parents, we often become our harshest critics, grappling with the lofty or societal expectations of motherhood and juggling the myriad other roles we play. But here's the thing: that mental load we bear, filled with all the "should haves" and "would haves," doesn't actually ever propel us forward. In fact, our proficiency in managing these tasks bears no relation to our worthiness of love and acceptance from our partners, our children, or ourselves.

FOSTER SELF-ACCEPTANCE

The reality of parental struggle is palpable, and it's crucial to acknowledge the impact of shame, blame, and the pursuit of perfection—not just on us but on our children, too. This understanding is vital from both the perspective of parental and educational expectations and the internal pressures our children place upon themselves. Often, in a school setting, attention is disproportionately given to children who are disruptive or exhibit noticeable behaviors. However, it's a poignant reminder for all of us to also be mindful of the quiet achievers, those who excel in silence. Do you have a child who takes immense pride in being the best at everything? Recognizing this trait is the first step. It's vital to understand how to support them in pursuing their goals while accepting the fact that they might not reach every single one of them.

It's about striking a balance—encouraging effort, resilience, and the joy of learning, rather than just the end result. When we shift our focus from perfection to personal growth, we help our children develop a healthier relationship with success and failure. It's about teaching them that every setback is an opportunity to learn and grow.

It's OK to not be perfect. Actually, there IS no perfect when it comes to living and emotional/mental health.

As parents, we set the tone for our children's behavior. By embracing our imperfections and treating ourselves with kindness and compassion, we model for our children that their worth isn't tied to their achievements (or their Pinterest-worthy bedroom). This approach not only alleviates the pressures they face but also fosters a nurturing environment where they can thrive, explore, and develop resilience. Remember, in the grand tapestry of life, it's the threads of effort, learning, and love that weave the most beautiful patterns.

> Growing up as the "golden child," my life was a portrait of achievement, each success painting a picture of a young woman who had it all together. But behind this façade of perfection, I was silently waging a battle with my own relentless standards. The quest for perfection in everything I did took a toll on my mental and emotional well-being. Anxiety became a constant companion, lurking in the shadows of each accomplishment, whispering doubts and fears.
>
> As I have come into my later adult years, I have relized that none of the achievements I was striving for gave me what I was seeking because I was bound by the core beliefs that keep me from connection to my truest selves. It's been a lifelong journey of understanding that perfection is not a prerequisite for worthiness, and in this realization, I found the first steps toward genuine self-acceptance and emotional freedom.
>
> —Kelly

When thinking about the concepts that children need to be taught to be able to understand self-acceptance and avoid perfectionism, there are two skills we want our children to be armed with:

- The knowledge that they don't need to do or be anything to be loved
- The ability to welcome and accept imperfections and trust they are worthy just as they are

For self-acceptance, the core beliefs that are being built are around self-worth and enough-ness.

SKILL: SELF-ACCEPTANCE

NEGATIVE BELIEF	POSITIVE BELIEF
I am bad	I am good enough
There is something wrong with me inside (I am defective)	I am good enough just the way I am
I am never good enough	I don't have to be perfect
I have to be something or do something to be loved	I am loved and accepted as I am
I am unlovable	I am lovable
It is not OK for me to mess up	It is OK for me to make mistakes

PROACTIVELY SUPPORTING SELF-ACCEPTANCE

Life has a way of giving us an abundance of chances to practice growth. When we make mistakes, we have an opportunity to learn new skills. When we feel down about ourselves, we have a chance to learn about our strengths and practice loving our attributes as they are.

This ability to practice self-acceptance and love ourselves even when things become tough is important for both kids and adults—but it's not always easy.

Fortunately, there are steps you can take to encourage a sense of self-acceptance in your child. If you're not already an expert at self-acceptance yourself, don't fret—most of these strategies can help you to learn the art of accepting yourself first. Then, you can be a model of self-acceptance and show your little one why it matters.

Self-acceptance is the state of accepting yourself for who you are without conditions or exceptions. In other words, it entails accepting your strengths and talents and your flaws and failures.

If you feel resistant to the idea of accepting your strengths and weaknesses, don't worry—you wouldn't be the first. It's easy to embrace positive traits, but accepting negative ones can feel uncomfortable. But once you accept your weaknesses, you can turn on your growth mindset and begin to learn from them. Self-acceptance is key in developing healthy self-esteem.

Self-acceptance is not a one-size-fits-all approach. In consideration of current systemic challenges, pressures, and issues, practicing self-acceptance is likely much easier said than done in many communities where families, friends, and kids are encouraged to overlook parts of their identity. However, this does not imply that self-acceptance should be disregarded—it may just require more time and reflection.

Self-acceptance creates the possibility for positive change by clarifying the areas you want to improve. Then, you can work to dissolve negative emotional blockages that may otherwise prevent you from getting there. Self-acceptance can also help you to become more accepting of others. As a parent or caregiver, learning how to accept your child for who they are can do wonders for them . . . and for your relationship with them.

The key to self-acceptance is understanding that you're not your actions, mistakes, or immutable characteristics. *You're so much more than that.*

Your worth as a person is essential. It is not dependent on you accomplishing certain milestones, looking a certain way, or being perfect. There's no single action or trait that can take your worth away from you. It's always there—you just need to know how to embrace it.

MODELING SELF-ACCEPTANCE WITH YOUR KIDS

As you can see, self-acceptance has a way of neutralizing difficult experiences and shedding light on the bigger picture. It reminds us that we're all flawed but that most of us are valiantly trying our best.

Even in the face of adversity, we deserve to love and honor our worth. We can also use our challenges to guide ourselves and our children in a better direction after accepting and learning from our mistakes.

Here, we'll explore five ways you can practice self-acceptance and show your kids how to do the same.

Accept the Things You Cannot Change

Showing your kids how to tell the difference between what's in their control and what isn't can help them to love themselves for who they are. By accepting and embracing their unique abilities and differences, they can feel more joy about themselves throughout their life.

Instead of lingering on the things they can't change, you can show your kids how to direct their efforts into growing and improving the things they *can* control.

Encourage Self-Forgiveness

We have all had moments that we aren't proud of—your child included. If your child is having a hard time accepting some of these moments and experiencing more negative emotions, they might be due for some self-forgiveness.

Teaching your child how to forgive themselves doesn't mean you're encouraging bad decisions or not showing them how to improve in the future. It simply means you're showing them how to free themselves from feeling bad about these past mistakes. Once you've forgiven yourself, you can be fully present. The present is the only place where positive changes can take place, after all.

Use Positive Affirmations for Self-Compassion

It's easy to feel down about yourself if you make a mistake or feel you can't control what's happening around you—and this goes for both kids and adults. To encourage self-acceptance in such times, you can help your child learn to show themselves compassion.

Self-compassion precedes many aspects of self-acceptance. Being compassionate toward yourself often involves treating and speaking to yourself as if you were your best friend. This type of self-talk may not come naturally to us or our children, but you can both practice it with the help of using positive affirmations for kids.

Affirmations are statements you repeat that express a sentiment you want to start embodying. Here are a few ideas for inspiration:

- "I am allowed to make mistakes and learn from them."
- "I am capable of making positive changes in my life."
- "I treat myself with love and respect."

Stop Comparing Yourself to Others

Some people say comparison is the thief of joy. The reason? No matter how amazing you are in your relationship, career, or finances—or for a child, a sport, a game, or a subject in school—there will always be someone who has you beat in a certain area.

Remind your child that their only job is to be the best version of themselves, rather than trying to be better than someone else. Do this by helping them make comparisons to their past self instead of friends or others around them. Here are some examples:

- Instead of saying "Wow! You scored more goals than Elijah!" after the game, say, "Wow! Your soccer skills are getting better every day."
- Instead of saying "Joanna is growing even taller than you!" say, "Look at that—you're an inch taller than you were last month!"

Practice, Practice, Practice

As with any new skill, learning self-acceptance might take practice. It might take some time for you and your kids to make self-acceptance into a habit, and it's OK if you find your inner critic shows up every now and again. In these moments, you can gently encourage your child to return to a place of self-acceptance.

The key is to be aware of when those feelings of negativity might come up—and actively show your kids how they can practice self-acceptance instead. This might happen during big life events, but you may find plenty of opportunities to practice in everyday tasks and moments. For example: "When something happens that your child can't change, help them see the positive side of things.

AFFIRMATION

I don't have to be perfect,
I can just be.
I am loved and enough
just by being me.

HOW TO SUPPORT PERFECTIONISM

Most of us don't love feeling guilt or shame so we find strategies to avoid these feelings. One of these strategies is perfectionism. Perfectionism is when parts of us want things to be just right in order to avoid some type of negative outcome. Sometimes what we are trying to avoid is internal self-blame; other times it's criticism or blame from others. Still other times it's because we are trying to avoid the disappointment of things not going as we had planned.

Here's the good news—the antidote to perfectionism is self-acceptance. And as we discussed, there are a number of ways to boost our self-acceptance skills. However, perfectionism and anxiety go hand in hand, and just as we work to improve self-acceptance, we should also be on the lookout for signs of anxiety. Here are some signs of perfectionism:

- Feeling badly about something unless the outcome is just as anticipated
- Difficulty starting tasks
- Procrastination
- Avoiding situations that could end in failure
- Being highly critical of yourself

Sometimes it can be hard to pick up on perfectionistic tendencies in young children. Younger children may show perfectionism less verbally and more in how they behave in certain situations. For instance:

- Having frequent meltdowns when they make a mistake
- Expressing embarrassment or shame when they get hurt
- Working hard to avoid disappointing others
- Struggling with making choices
- Avoiding trying new things or starting tasks
- Constantly asking for adult help for tasks they are able to do themselves

To be clear, these signs need to be taken in context as there are other reasons children may show these behaviors, but it can be helpful to begin to notice what is triggering to each child. If it seems like your child's behaviors are tied to "making mistakes" or having things be "just so," you may be witnessing perfectionistic tendencies. If you notice these things early, you can start to support children to learn self-acceptance.

AFFIRMATION

I am loved as I am.
When things get tough,
I go back to my heart.
I know I'm enough.

Parent Reflection Moment: Self-Acceptance

Whether you are struggling with your own feelings of enough-ness or you notice your child struggling with feeling like they aren't good enough, we recommend having a moment to connect with Self.

Here are some questions to consider if you would like to implement our CALM Moment with a focus on Self-Acceptance. You can return to Chapter 5, pages 98–100 ("CALM Moments") to have an outline of this process as you engage in the following Reflection Questions.

In moments of struggle, when seeking clarity and self-comfort, ponder these questions:

- Consider the ways you might be being hard on yourself. How can you cultivate more self-compassion and acceptance?

- Think about what your child is currently struggling with. How can you offer a supportive presence, accepting all their emotions in this challenging time?

For broader reflection on self-acceptance and dealing with perfectionism:

- Explore what practices or thoughts help you in being more accepting of yourself.
- Reflect on the messages you received in childhood about conditions of being loved and consider if any of these beliefs still influence you.
- Assess your expectations of being a "perfect" parent and how these might be impacting you.
- When you face difficulty in self-acceptance, identify what you truly need in those moments. Consider if your child might benefit from similar support.

Things to Remember

- Make sure to praise your child's efforts, not just the outcome.
- Model for your child that perfection isn't necessary and mistakes are learning opportunities.
- Encourage your child to express their feelings about challenges and failures and validate their emotions.

SLUMBERKINS CHARACTER CONNECTION: YAK

CHAPTER 15

Conflict Resolution

W e always say "welcome all feelings" in the world of Slumberkins. So much so, it's the title of this book. But what does it mean to actually welcome *mad* feelings? Most of us grew up in an era where being mad was "bad." We were ordered to stomp off to our rooms alone, or an equally mad or posturing parent announced that they would "tame" our mad feelings for us if we couldn't regulate them ourselves.

Conflict resolution refers to the skills and factors involved in solving and resolving conflict. But before we can dive into how to support kids through conflicts, we first need to address the components of conflict—anger, emotion regulation, and repair—and break them down individually.

THE COMPONENTS OF CONFLICT

Anger is a particularly tricky emotion. As a parent, you may feel helpless watching your child attempt to cope with anger, whether it leads to a big expression of the feeling (like a tantrum) or not. Even infants express anger, like when they don't want to be picked up or something feels uncomfortable. Especially as your child grows older, you might feel scared or overwhelmed or unsafe when you watch them feel anger.

There can be an intensity to the feeling of anger because of the reaction we have to it. Culturally, we place an extreme focus on anger, both in controlling it and in making it disappear.

There's more to anger than you might think, though. Anger is a secondary emotion, an expression that occurs when there is an underlying need that has not been met. Kids who are throwing tantrums aren't just angry for the sake of being angry. They're disappointed about something, they're sad that things didn't go their way, or they're surprised in a negative way. The only way to work through sadness or disappointment or shock is to sit with those feelings, which can be tough to do.

Instead, they get angry. Anger is almost an antidote. It's easier to feel anger because that means you're *doing* something and pushing forward in some way rather than just sitting with the feeling; getting angry gives you a release. But ignoring the underlying cause of that anger can lead to negative patterns of behavior. Even so, parents should not feel obligated to eliminate anger in their children. It is not your responsibility to "fix" your child's feelings. Your job is to create a safe space for them to feel their feelings.

> It is not your responsibility to "fix" your child's feelings. Your job is to create a safe space for them to feel their feelings.
>
> —Kelly

You do, however, need to be mindful of your own reaction to your child's anger and how you support—or don't support—them showing, feeling, or expressing it in a healthy way.

As children grow and their capacity for coping with their emotions changes, they're looking at you to model how to handle tricky emotions, and sometimes when it feels like they're "exploding" in front of you, they're really just saying, "Help me figure this out!"

Of course knowing this intellectually and coping with this in the moment are two different things. So let's take a look at how children express anger at different stages.

Once something happens to challenge a child's belief about the role of anger in their life, there are two skills or concepts we want to teach our children:

- Knowing that mad feelings are OK and safe to express
- How to take care of their mad feelings first and then repair after conflict

For conflict resolution, the core beliefs that are being built are around emotional safety and lovability.

SKILL: ANGER, EMOTION REGULATION, REPAIR & CONFLICT RESOLUTION

NEGATIVE BELIEF	POSITIVE BELIEF
Mad is bad	Mad is not bad
Only "good" feelings are OK	All feelings are welcome
I am bad	We all make mistakes
I deserve to be alone	I am worthy of love and connection (even when I make mistakes)
My feelings are wrong	My feelings are valid
I can't control my reactions	I can learn healthy ways to get my needs met

DEALING WITH TANTRUMS

Tantrums are behaviors that are a manifestation of a deeper emotion or unmet need. They're the tip of the iceberg, so to speak. Below the tantrum lies anger, and below the anger lies the primary emotion—sadness, disappointment, surprise.

Remind yourself that tantrums are not personal. Your child has an underlying need and wants to communicate. It just so happens that they are attempting to communicate in a tantrum-y way. Instead of being bogged down by your own embarrassment that you have the only four-year-old who can't seem to behave at a formal event, step back and try to assess the issue. Holding a bit of distance between the behavior and your reaction will help resolve the issue faster.

As a teacher, I can step back from a tantrum and more easily assess why this child is exhibiting this type of behavior. As a parent, it is much, much harder.

—Callie

The behaviors coming from your own child are *the* most triggering for you, which is why parenting becomes its own journey of emotional growth and developmental milestones for you.

—Kelly

Focus on Co-regulation

When a child is having a tantrum, don't even bother trying to use logic—at least, not at first.

Instead, model the state you would like them to eventually arrive at. Sit calmly, take deep breaths, and be patient as they work some of their angry energy out of their body. All of the intense things that might be happening—kicking, screaming, flailing—are a visual representation for you of what's going on inside for them. It's not about you as an adult. It's about them being completely out of control.

Co-regulation is a supportive practice between children and adults helping children learn to regulate their own feelings. When a child is in the middle of an anger outburst, sometimes talking with them won't be effective. Instead, try to focus on safety. As long as your child isn't hurting themselves or others, it's best to let the tantrum wind down in appropriate ways. Co-regulating might look like:

Containment: Moving your child to a space where they are safe. Try to keep your child away from sharp objects like counters, tables, stairs, and such. If you're at home, their room is often the most calming and safe setting. If you're in public, try to guide your child to an area without hazards such as cars, bystanders, or other kids, if possible. Your car may provide a safe, closed space where you can let them sit and decompress. Through containment, you are telling your child, "I'm not going to let you be unsafe. I am here to keep you safe and help you make safe choices."

Be silent: When your child is in the middle of a tantrum, direct confrontations aren't helpful. Raising your voice will only create more stress and agitation. Instead, stay close by to ensure their safety, but allow the tantrum to wind down without engaging. By talking, you can retrigger the anger.

Wait it out: A dim, quiet space is ideal for settling an overstimulated child. If possible, lower the lights, turn off the TV, and ask siblings to leave the room. Pause until you're at a place where you feel a loving connection again.

Create a designated safe zone: If your child has angry outbursts regularly, it can help to plan ahead by creating an area that's set up for self-soothing. Make a comfort corner in their room or the living room the "safe zone." Outfit it with items your child finds comforting, like a special stuffie for hugging, a weighted blanket, or a curtain for privacy and minimizing light.

I might have thought my son Oli was loud as a baby, but through the toddler years and today as a seven-year-old, his expression of anger can get *big*. The energy can fill up a whole room and feel quite overwhelming to try to "welcome."

Sometimes it looks like holding him to keep safe and just breathing with him. I've also had to sit across the room from him while he was throwing pieces of paper at me, which I only accepted because he was no longer throwing books. Again, I had to remind myself to take breaths to calm my own nervous system so that I could stay by his side to prove that he's not alone with his mad feelings.

Over time, we've built trust and emotional safety, and he knows I'll keep him company. Usually after 15 minutes of sitting with him in the room (which can honestly feel like a long time), just breathing, and taking care of my nervous system, I can help Oli get to a calmer place.

Once he is in a calm place, I still don't try to jump to repair or solve whatever got us here in the first place. We simply just sit with the emotions, together. Honestly, he usually comes around once he is calm and has a true apology and expresses how much he didn't like being out of control like that.

—Kelly

WHY "GO TO YOUR ROOM!" WON'T WORK

We've all been there. Your six-year-old lashes out and hits your eight-year-old for taking the "best" seat at the dinner table. Your immediate reaction is to yell, "We don't hit! Go to your room!"

Why do we have that reaction? Probably because that's what we heard our parents say to us when we were young. On the surface, it makes sense. You are bringing the negative behavior to a complete halt by physically removing the child from the scene of the conflict. The child has time and space to reflect on the behavior, and then they can rejoin the family, leaving the issue in the past.

But it doesn't work.

When we were young, anger and sadness were two things that weren't welcome emotions in many houses. They had to be felt in isolation or be hidden away.

—Callie

Here's what could happen in that scenario.

- Internalized anger: The feeling of being "sent away" from the family in this circumstance teaches them that anger has to be shut down because it is not a welcome emotion. When children are left alone with feelings, it can lead to beliefs that manifest in behaviors that are self-harming or dangerous. Or at the very least, they can lead to anger outbursts as adults.
- Externalized anger: A child who doesn't have the ability to regulate themselves may inadvertently harness their anger to control others. It is common for them to turn that anger outward to create a world in which everything feels better to them and they can feel safe and stable. They may exhibit anger toward others as a sort of "bully" in order to maintain control.

COMMUNICATION DURING TANTRUMS

How you communicate before, during, and after an anger episode is key to teaching your child to manage anger appropriately, as well as how to repair after an episode. Try these techniques if your child's anger feels big and loud and out of control.

You know your child better than anyone. If you start to suspect that something feels off in terms of their expressions of anger, you might consider looking for answers. If you feel like you need extra support, a therapist may be able to help you fine-tune your own parent super-powers. They'll ask questions and help you dig into what might really be going on. Trust your gut. If you suspect you might need extra help, ask for it. Never feel ashamed or embarrassed. You're doing a good job—a great job—by asking for support.

At the end of the day, make sure that you're tuned in to your child. Help them navigate what feels best for them in terms of growth and connection and understanding, and seek support for anything that feels above and beyond your ability. Making small shifts may help improve your family life.

When your child is calm, have a talk about your expectations for behavior and what happens if those boundaries aren't followed.

Talk with your child about what they were feeling before they got angry. Was there something they wanted? Were they feeling lonely or bored? As you identify the situations that trigger your child, talk with them about how they can respond to that trigger differently next time.

It can be tempting to adjust your behavior to avoid triggering your child. But by trying to change your actions to keep your child calm, you're inadvertently showing them that tantrums work.

Address Destructive Behavior

When anger escalates to the point of being destructive or dangerous, it's challenging to know how to respond. While you don't want to validate the tantrum by giving in, you also need to minimize harm.

When tantrums become destructive, step in to prevent injury. If your child is throwing, hitting, punching, or flailing their arms, you may need to physically restrain them to prevent injury. Be gentle, but firm: "I can't let you hit/throw/hurt yourself."

If your child's anger is frequent and uncontrollable, consider seeking outside help. Family therapy can be very helpful if you feel that your child's rage is destructive and causing harm to your family.

Avoiding Escalation During Outbursts

Reasoning with your child during a rage isn't going to be effective, and it's likely to make you feel more frustrated. There are two reasons this often doesn't work.

Instead of reasoning or arguing, give your child clear, short directions while an outburst is occurring ("Take a deep breath" or "Let's go to your comfort corner"). Keep your tone even and calm. Wait for them to calm down before trying to talk about the problem.

AFFIRMATION

*I can be mad
and let my feelings show.
I will always be loved
in my heart, I know.*

SIBLING RIVALRY

If you have more than one child, you've likely experienced sibling rivalry at some point. You might have even experienced it in the last 10 minutes. It might be arguing over toys or games, fighting over food, name-calling, or even physical scuffles. In many families, it's all of the above. Although sibling rivalry can be tough to handle, it's important to remember that some degree of strife between sibs is perfectly normal. In fact, sibling relationships are where children develop foundational social skills like negotiating compromise, setting boundaries, and considering other perspectives. However, when sibling conflict gets out of hand, it can lead to problems in your family dynamic.

Although conflict between your children can feel stressful, in most cases, sibling rivalry is nothing to fear. Sibling relationships play a critical role in early childhood social emotional learning and development, and conflict is a normal part of human interactions.

PEER CONFLICT

We have unique viewpoints and perspectives as educators and parents: we see and understand the different social dynamics at play when a conflict may arise. We know from experience that if your child is struggling with peer conflict in school, you should get involved with the teacher or school counselor as soon as possible. Over-communicate with them and get their insight into the situation. It truly takes a village, and the more you and the school staff are on the same team to support your child, the better. Those of our students whose parents were closely connected to the interventions we put in place at school and also supported them in a similar way at home made further progress and achieved their goals in the school environment smoother and faster than if parents weren't involved.

It can be very hard to know where to start, though.

I was teaching in my own classroom when I received a call that any teacher would dread. My son Henry, who was a kindergartner at the time, was in her office and completely verbally shut down, unable to participate in a conversation about a conflict that had happened on the playground between him and his best friend.

The playground had two swings. Henry was unwilling to get off a swing when his best friend told him it was finally his turn. It ended in a scuffle with some bark dust being kicked and big emotions being expressed between the two.

Even though Henry wasn't the one with the big reaction in this situation, he was not able to engage in the process of repair after the conflict very easily.

This whole experience of wanting to empower and equip our students as well as our own kids (like Henry in this situation) led us to write the book *Hammerhead's Recess Challenge*. It provides both sides of the conflict with a framework for repair so that the kids aren't stuck in conflict, causing longer lasting reactivity or difficulty with peers than needed.

It helps kids take accountability for big reactions without shame, and it provides space for reconnection.

Through its affirmation, Hammerhead attempts to give children a template for apology and repair in order to keep children supported in their peer groups, even when their regulation or behavior might make it difficult.

I've used this affirmation and story time and time again with my own kids, and it continues to be one of our most popular stories for educators to use in their classrooms. Henry, now a middle schooler, loves the fact that he inspired Hammerhead, and there are moments when I can see him trying to step into the "wise older brother" mentor role with his younger siblings, sharing his experience and story with them.

—Callie

If you pick up your child from school or arrive home to find them upset, it's best to try to maintain your own composure so that you can be a steady presence for them to rely on. Then, ask them to tell you what happened, step-by-step.

Even if you suspect your child did something to violate another child's boundary, saying kind things like "I understand how that must have felt" can help reinforce their sense that they're supported.

AFFIRMATION

I felt mad, now I'm calm. I can use my words instead.
I'm sorry I hurt you, I still want to be friends.

PARENT REFLECTION MOMENT: CONFLICT RESOLUTION

Conflict is one of the most common reasons for parents needing to take a break and soothe their own system. When you feel like you are going to lose your cool, try checking in with yourself, calming down, and bringing that calm energy and insight back into your parenting.

Here are some questions to consider if you would like to implement our CALM Moment with a focus on Conflict Resolution. You can return to Chapter 5, pages 98–100 ("CALM Moments") to have an outline of this process as you engage in the following.

In moments of struggle, when seeking clarity and self-comfort, ponder these questions:

- Are there ways in which you're feeling overstimulated, such as loud noises or intense behavior from your child? Think about what you need to maintain safety and lead effectively in these situations.
- Identify what is being triggered within you. Is your child exhibiting behavior that you were not allowed to express as a child? Explore why this may be triggering for you.
- Consider what your child might be trying to communicate through their behavior. How can you interpret this as a call for your assistance? What does your child need from you at this moment?

For broader reflection on conflict resolution:

- Reflect on your family's approach to anger and how it was handled during your childhood.
- Think about your emotions when you need to apologize or engage in a repair process. Was this something modeled in your home?
- Identify the behaviors from your child that trigger you the most and consider what these behaviors might be communicating.

Things to Remember

- "Mad" is not "bad," and in fact anger is an essential part of emotional development.
- Co-regulation is the healthiest way for parents to help children process anger.
- Sibling rivalry and peer conflict are bound to occur. Remember to step back, demonstrate empathy, and avoid trying to "fix" the problem.

SLUMBERKINS CHARACTER CONNECTION: HAMMERHEAD

CHAPTER 16

Change

Humans are creatures of habit. Knowing that we'll have a cup of coffee each morning or that we'll scroll on our phones at night before we go to bed creates a predictable, soothing pattern that helps organize our days. Kids thrive on consistency, too, whether it's drinking milk every morning or reading a book with you every night. That's why we talked a lot about the importance of building routines, structure, and predictability in Chapter 2, "Stages of Emotional Development." Now we're going to talk about what happens when that routine, structure, and predictability all comes crashing down.

One thing is certain: change happens constantly, both around us and within us. While we might yearn for prolonged moments of comfort and stability, life teaches us that things rarely stay the same for long. This flux is not only external, in the world around us, but also internal, in the evolving needs and development of both ourselves and our children. Changes may be minor, like losing a tooth, or major, like moving to a new city or going through a divorce. To cope and adapt to change, we need to learn to be resilient. Being prepared to navigate changes for yourself while also parenting your children is a necessary skill to have in your toolbox.

SUPPORTING CHANGE IN CHILDREN'S LIVES

As adults, we each find our unique ways to adapt to change, some methods healthier than others. Yet, it is through the lens of parenthood that we truly comprehend the impact of change. Observing our children confront and adapt to changes, we're reminded of how overwhelming and disorienting these shifts can be, especially in a world that feels vast and complex to their young minds.

Because our parents didn't necessarily raise us with the emotional skills needed to process change, we might not be completely prepared to help guide our children. Instead of thinking of that as a shortfall, consider it an opportunity to learn, grow, and develop alongside our children, helping them navigate life's inevitable change with grace.

As a school counselor, I hosted a "Family Change" group to support children who were experiencing all kinds of big changes—the most common being a divorce, but there were also children in foster homes or military families on active duty.

I knew that the kids I was working with needed to hear messages of support from their parents or primary caregivers. This is key to helping children form positive core beliefs. This knowledge is part of what inspired us to write the book *Fox's Big Family Change*. Within the book, we integrated some simple and helpful things parents and caregivers could do with their children to support them through these big changes.

One of those things we stressed was addressing the change in a very straightforward way, focusing on what would change and what would not.

Then, we narrowed in on the emotions of their child, helping parents develop a healthy curiosity for what their children were feeling while also allowing them space for emotional expression.

I also knew kids needed to hear a key phrase: "It's not your fault." This phrase is essential because whenever there is a big family change like divorce, kids tend to think the change is because of something they did. Make sure to have that explicit and direct conversation with your child so they hear those words directly from you. Even if you say it only once.

—Kelly

When thinking about supporting changes in our child's lives, there are two skills or concepts that we want to teach our children:

- They are supported and safe to feel all of the feelings when change happens
- How to cope and know that big changes are not their fault

When change happens, the core beliefs that are being formed are concepts of emotional safety and responsibility.

SKILL: COPING WITH CHANGE

NEGATIVE BELIEF	POSITIVE BELIEF
I am alone	I am not alone
I can't get through this	I can get through hard times
I have to be a certain way to be loved	All my feelings are welcome
It's my fault things changed	It's not my fault that things changed
I need to protect myself and can't share my feelings	I can stay open to new things
Change is bad	New is different, not always bad

LEARNING ABOUT FAMILY SYSTEMS

As we delve into the realm of family dynamics and their response to change, it's crucial to understand the insights offered by research on family systems. Dr. Murray Bowen was a psychiatrist who helped lay out how complex family systems really are. His research and theory were foundational to the work, training, and influence of family systems and supports. Much research has been done about family systems, and there is a lot of information and ideas about this complex topic. We are going to try to synthesize what we have come to understand from our training and lived experiences.

All families are systems, and when something happens, the system changes. All sorts of changes can affect a family and how it functions. Changes include welcoming a new baby, a toddler learning to walk, moving into a new developmental stage, starting a new job, moving to a new city, getting a divorce, or losing a loved one.

Signs of a Healthy Family System

These are the signs of a healthy family system:

- Members feel safe to express their thoughts and feelings, knowing they will be met with understanding and respect.
- Families can navigate changes, whether big or small, by coming together, discussing, and adapting to new circumstances collaboratively.
- They are adaptable to change and open to modifying family rules and roles when needed.
- There's a strong sense of support and understanding among family members.

Signs That a Family System Is Not Functioning Well

Family systems that struggle to function effectively often display certain signs, particularly during times of change. These can include:

- Family members may struggle to express themselves or feel unheard. There might be a pattern of misunderstanding and assumption.
- There may be a strict adherence to roles and rules, regardless of changing circumstances.
- Family members either avoid addressing issues, leading to unresolved tensions, or frequently have intense conflicts without resolution.
- Members may be overly involved in each other's lives, lacking healthy boundaries (enmeshment), or conversely, there may be a lack of connectedness and emotional support (disengagement).

- There may be a tendency to blame others for problems in the family, or a lack of accountability for individual actions.
- You may observe a general sense of stress, anxiety, or unhappiness pervading family interactions, especially during times of change.

Family therapists are trained to understand children from a family systems perspective. That means that although we recognize the innate uniqueness of each individual, we look at the context of the family system in which a child is living to understand them better. Sometimes, things that appear to be a problem with a child (like attention-seeking behavior or acting out) can actually be a strategy for coping with an issue within the family system. It always helps to understand the whole picture of a child's life to understand their behavior, especially in the early years.

Occasionally, larger underlying family issues need to be addressed prior to working on a child's behavior. This is often the case in families with mental health or addiction issues. For example, when the person with the issue finds support through therapy or rehab, the child is able to have more space, presence, and attunement from other family members, often resulting in diminished behaviors for the child. It's also a step toward a healthier functioning family system as a whole.

—Kelly

There are many situations that cause big changes for families. We are going to narrow in on some of the most common ones that we talk about and that we have the best tools and support for.

INTRODUCING A NEW SIBLING

Welcoming a new baby to the family is hard enough for parents—but imagine how much more complicated it would seem if you were still a child! Luckily, many activities and strategies can help with preparing kids for a new baby by promoting feelings of inclusion during this major change and family transition.

As a parent about to bring a new little person into the mix, it can be hard to predict how your first child or older kids will respond. Getting ready for a new sibling can feel like a highwire act: the balance of their feelings with the reality that life as they know it is about to change forever. Fortunately, there are tons of creative (and fun) ways to help your kids process the idea that a new sibling is on the way.

As you prepare to dive into that initial conversation, take a beat and try to put yourself in their little sneakers. Depending on their age, some kids won't be able to understand what having a younger sibling around will be like. Don't be surprised if their initial reaction is one of indifference.

On the other hand, some slightly older kids may respond with feelings of anger or frustration. They may worry their parents won't have time for them or focus on practical details like where the newborn baby will sleep and whether they'll have to share their toys with them.

All of these reactions are normal. When a child finds out that their family of three is about to become a family of four (or more!), they're likely to experience big feelings about it—but not necessarily right away. These feelings may manifest as expressions of sadness, joy, fear, surprise, or grief.

During this time, it's important to make sure your child feels heard and that their emotions are being considered. Spend time talking to them about what they're feeling. Make sure to pile on the positive attention to show them they are loved. You can also help mitigate their anxiety by talking to them about the baby in ways that soothe their worries and help them feel included.

Children are still learning to process information and begin to understand the world around them. But at this point, many kids aren't able to think with adult-aged logic—or find the words to express what they're feeling. To match their processing timeline, preparing your kids to greet a whole new human being will probably require several conversations, rather than one big one. To get the ball rolling, these three activities can help you meet them where they're at.

Understanding a Toddler's Reaction to a New Sibling

Despite your best efforts, there will be moments when your toddler expresses frustration, fear, or anger over your pregnancy and the newborn baby on the way. Don't be alarmed if it's not all excitement all the time. After all, you're probably cycling through your own sequence of anxiety and elation.

Research shows that the introduction of a new baby can be a stressful event in the life of a young child. Common behavior responses include clinginess, jealousy, withdrawal, or seeking attention. These initial reactions could feel negative—especially in light of reduced sleep, feeding difficulties, and all the other stressors that come with caring for a newborn. If you can, try to reframe these responses as important indicators to pay attention to.

Strong expressions of emotion from your toddler may not always feel pleasant, but they are valid signals of how well your child is coping with the process of becoming a sibling. Keeping the following guidelines in mind can help them (and you) navigate the transition.

Don't Assume They're Excited

Many toddlers express enthusiasm about being a big brother or big sister early in the process. However, those feelings may be distant in those first moments when they're able to imagine seeing their sibling in the bassinet. This is perfectly normal.

Validate their emotions by asking them what they're feeling early and often. This shows them that you're a reliable container for them to express what they're feeling, from jealousy to joy.

As for *your* emotions? It's not uncommon to find yourself experiencing anxiety or disappointment when they get frustrated around the baby. Be gentle with yourself and try to remember these feelings are complicated and will likely ebb and flow as your child adapts.

To support any change, this simple sheet is an example of how to help kids process the changes and communicate their thoughts and perspectives about the change to you as a parent.

AFFIRMATION

When change happens,
I know what to do.
I welcome my feelings
and trust I'll get through.

SEPARATION AND DIVORCE

If you're navigating a divorce, worries about the impact on your child can be one of the most stressful parts of the experience. For decades, we've heard that research on divorce and children shows that divorce is harmful to a child's well-being. However, this isn't always the case. In fact, divorce itself isn't the problem—strife between divorced parents and caregivers is what can hurt children's emotional health.

Additionally, the way society may stigmatize divorce or view and treat families navigating divorce can have an impact on young children. For example, the term "broken home" has a negative connotation, and children may internalize these types of labels based on what those around them are saying. Therefore, it's important to have conversations with your kids about your separation and let them know you'll support them every step of the way so they can internalize their own understanding of the situation.

Still, divorce is a life-altering event that can affect your child's future and relationships. But not to worry. There are many ways you can make divorce easier for your child. The end of a marriage can be the beginning of a positive new chapter in your lives where you can establish strong connections with your child and encourage positive co-parenting.

How to Explain Divorce to Kids

The first step to creating an open dialogue around divorce is explaining it to your children. Many caregivers fear they won't know how to answer all of their child's questions. But you don't need to have all the answers right away. All you need to do is have an honest, loving, and age-appropriate conversation.

Be honest about the situation: As best you can, try to answer questions truthfully and without bias. Your children need to feel they can trust you. Remember, they're likely already well aware of the parental stress and tension in the household leading up to the separation or divorce. It's important they feel included in the changes taking place.

Avoid placing blame: Do not blame one parent or the other. Reassure your child that both parents still love them. It's essential to explain that both parents will still be involved in their lives, even though they may not live together anymore. Your child needs to know that their own relationship with their parents won't change.

Emphasize that your child is not to blame: Children of divorce often worry that their behavior caused fighting, or even made one parent want to leave. Reassure your child that they are not responsible in any way for issues between their parents.

Make space for their feelings: You're experiencing a lot of pain too, but it's vital to allow your child to express their emotions without fear of upsetting you. Allow them to ask questions and express their feelings while you actively listen and validate their emotions. Process your own feelings about the divorce with friends, family, or a therapist.

Impacts of the Parental Relationship on Children

In the past, researchers believed this meant that parental divorce causes harm to children. However, more modern studies have found that these problems come from the stress between parents that leads to divorce—not divorce itself.

Even so, many signs of stress can be found in children of divorced parents and households, such as behavioral problems, school issues, depression, and low self-esteem.

Whether caregivers are openly fighting with each other or giving each other the silent treatment, children feel the tension all the same. This parental conflict and strife at home causes behavior problems and mental health conditions such as anxiety, depression, sleep problems, poor school performance, and more.

In situations like this, divorce is a short-term stressor that leads to a happier, healthier home life in the long run. In fact, once children from divorced homes have adjusted to the change, they have fewer emotional and behavioral problems than children in high-conflict, married homes.

There are five key factors that make divorce more or less psychologically damaging for children:

- Level of conflict between the parents, exposure to conflict, and perception of conflict resolution between parents
- Mental health of the parents
- Involvement of the nonprimary caregiver
- Financial impact
- The child's perception of events

Some of these factors are outside of your control, such as the financial impact of divorcing. But you can work with your co-parent to minimize as many of these factors as you can.

Parenting through a divorce is painful. It's heavy, and it's full of questions, changes, and all the feelings. Looking back on it now, I'm not sure how I did it. I was definitely functioning in survival mode for about a year.

What I tried my best at was holding space for sadness and grief of the loss of the family unit with the kids. This was incredibly difficult.

Yet it's one of the most healing things I've had to do for myself, too.

This process has looked different for each of my children. I have one child who is deeply sensitive and feels and expresses *everything*. If he's sad, I know it, so I will openly welcome it. I just kind of sit in the emotion with him. Every time, though, once he's all cried out and is ready to move on, I need a little self-check to regroup for myself. Sitting in the emotion with him activates the sad and guilty feelings that I am holding back.

My third child—the youngest of the bunch—doesn't hold as many memories of what life was like with us as a family unit, but she often articulates a feeling that there's something missing and her heart feels heavy. Noticing that she was saying that pretty regularly, I paid attention to when it was happening; it always seemed to happen at bedtime on the nights after a transition back from her dad's house.

When she shares these feelings with me, I remind myself what's really going on: she's processing grief over the family unit she knew as a younger child. I'll usually start with getting curious and asking her what she needs, and if she doesn't know, I offer some solutions like talking more about it, a hug or cuddles, or some space. Most often she just wants a back rub and snuggles, but recently, she replied, "I'll take some space. I just need to be with me."

I have another child who is an internalizer. He has a hard time with communication and verbally articulating his feelings about the harder things. He was older when the divorce happened—and the kids would never have known anything was wrong in the marriage—so the shock of the change and dealing with something that was completely out of his control was really difficult. . .and it still is. We are working with a therapist because I needed help to support him, even with all of the resources in my toolbox.

It can be incredibly difficult to know that you can't will your kids to be emotionally well or do the work for them, especially since you're carrying the weight of making an adult decision that impacts their lives so deeply. But meeting them where they are and just simply being with them in connection as we navigate through has become the new normal.

—Callie

Looking Ahead to Co-Parenting

Families come in all shapes and sizes, but any time they change—as in the event of a separation or divorce—the fracture will inevitably affect the whole family. Co-parenting means working collaboratively to provide your child with an environment where they can feel safe, secure, and encouraged to bond with both parents equally.

Knowing how to co-parent, however, will work differently for every family. Understanding the options for establishing a copacetic, child-first arrangement can help each of you navigate current and future adjustments successfully.

While you may have different parenting styles, it's a good idea to agree on some basic rules for raising your child with consistency between households. The more communicative and aligned you can be as co-parents, the less margin there is for either party to blur lines or cause your child distress.

Whatever your separation circumstances, aim to agree upon:

- Custody and visitation schedules
- Your child's education and healthcare
- Holidays and extended family involvement
- The best way to stay in touch (like phone calls)

Whether you work it out yourselves or with the guidance of an attorney, having a co-parenting agreement plan will help to minimize conflicts and create a sense of security for your child.

AFFIRMATION

I am safe, I am loved.
I can get through this part.
It's not my fault that things changed,
and I can keep an open heart.

PARENT REFLECTION MOMENT: CHANGE

Change in the family can be stressful for adults and children alike. If you are in a big-feelings moment or if you are just dealing with high levels of stress or change on a daily basis, take a moment to check in with yourself.

C—Center Yourself Begin by grounding yourself in the present. Take a few slow, deep breaths, and you may find it helpful to close your eyes and place your hands on your heart or belly. Use this time to slow down your body, clear your mind, and soothe your system. Recognize and name your feelings and the thoughts that are arising.

Here are some questions to consider if you would like to implement our CALM Moment with a focus on change. You can return to Chapter 5, pages 98–100 ("CALM Moments") to have an outline of this process as you engage in the following Reflection Questions.

In moments of struggle, when seeking clarity and self-comfort, ponder these questions:

- Ask yourself what your feelings are trying to communicate to you at this moment.
- Consider what your child's feelings might be trying to convey.

For broader reflection on family change:

- Reflect on significant changes you experienced as a child and what support you wished for from the adults in your life.
- Think about your general reactions to change and the strategies that help you adjust.
- Contemplate how your child copes with change and what might assist them in managing and adjusting to their feelings about it.

M—Move Forward with Intention Now, it's time to move forward with intention based on your reflections and understanding. Decide on a course of action that addresses both your needs and those of your child. This could involve adopting new coping strategies, facilitating open conversations about change, or implementing supportive measures to ease the transition. Remember, moving forward means taking proactive steps that honor the emotional well-being of both you and your child. (For further guidance on taking action, refer to Chapter 5, "The Connect-to-Grow Approach in Practice.")

Things to Remember

- Though kids thrive on consistency, helping them learn to adapt to change builds resilience.
- Watching your children navigate change can be disorienting to you as a parent, so you need to remember to take care of your own feelings along with supporting your children.
- Practice patience. It will take time for your child—and you!—to adjust to a big change.

SLUMBERKINS CHARACTER CONNECTION: FOX

CHAPTER 17

Anxiety

Anxiety has become present in so many of our lives in an ever-changing world. It is part of the reality we face daily as humans, and especially as parents, and it's affecting our kids. We know we've said it before, but in this instance it is especially important to understand that our child's emotional wellness is not separate from our own—even more so in the early years of infancy and childhood. It highlights the need to be aware of when and how anxiety shows up for you as an adult as you navigate your role as a parent.

Anxiety is often perceived as an unwelcome guest or a constant nagging enemy. We assume that if the anxiety would just go away, things would be OK. Worrisome, spiraling thoughts or fears that can oftentimes be very difficult to control show up and take control of our minds. Sometimes it's incredibly tricky to see things clearly, and other times it can be downright crippling. When we start to observe those same thoughts, fears, and patterns surface in our own kids, it can be even harder to know how to support them while coping with our own fears, too.

WHAT IF WE REFRAME ANXIETY?

What if we learn that anxiety actually holds a significant adaptive purpose in our internal systems and our lives? In fact, it's showing up to play a very important role—anxiety is our protector.

Picture anxiety as a vigilant guardian in your mind. Its original role, deeply rooted in our evolutionary history, was to protect us from danger. This ancient mechanism, like an internal alarm system, alerts us to potential threats, ensuring our survival. In modern times we face fewer physical dangers, but this system still activates in response to any kind of perceived threat—physical, emotional, or social.

For children, anxiety can manifest as a response to new or challenging situations, like starting school, taking a test, or navigating friendships. This emotional response is not inherently negative; rather, it's a sign that the child's mind is engaged and alert, processing potential risks and preparing to handle them. It's a natural part of their emotional learning journey.

In its balanced form, anxiety encourages children to be cautious and thoughtful, to prepare adequately for upcoming challenges, and to learn from their surroundings. It's a catalyst for developing problem-solving skills, fostering resilience, and building confidence through overcoming fears.

However, like any emotion, anxiety needs to be understood and supported. It's important for parents and caregivers to recognize when anxiety is serving its purpose and when it may become overwhelming or is on unnecessary overdrive. By acknowledging and talking about anxiety—and what is going on for it to come online as a protector openly—we can teach children how to navigate this emotion, differentiate between realistic and unrealistic fears, and develop coping strategies.

It took some years for me to truly understand the difference between stress and anxiety. I don't think I even heard the word *anxiety* in my house growing up, and yet it was ever present. *Stress* and *pressure* were common words, and they were often used around performance and achievement with school and sports. I went to college on an athletic scholarship, which added layers of pressure to perform.

It wasn't until I had kids that I truly became acquainted with anxiety.

I've personified the part of me that gets anxious as an overprotective, deeply loyal friend, who will never back down until she knows for a fact that things are emotionally safe and under control.

Anxiety-with-a-capital-A showed up with a vengeance, especially after my daughter was born. It took me a couple of years to understand that anxious thoughts and fears were flooding me and taking control of my system. Eventually, I learned that I was experiencing premenstrual dysphoric disorder (PMDD) and postpartum anxiety. Combined, those two issues led me on a path to understand what was going on for me because it was affecting every aspect of my life—my relationship with my spouse, my friendships, my work at Slumberkins, my ability to parent the way I wanted to. It was a slow burn, but a couple of years down the road, things really went south.

One day I met a friend for lunch, and as we were catching up and I was telling them all about Slumberkins and life in general, I had a realization. It dawned on me that even though I know all the things and I cofounded a children's emotional wellness brand, I, myself, was not actually well. There's a stark difference between *knowing* about social and emotional skills and actually *being* emotionally well.

The next day, I found a therapist and started on a path of trying to figure it out *because I had to*. There was no other choice.

It's been six years since that lightbulb conversation. I now can reflect back and recognize that my anxiety was running my life at the time; it was setting off alarm bells left and right, and I was completely ignoring them. I had suppressed my intuition and spent years doing the things I "should do" while ignoring so many gut feelings. I was self-abandoning all over the place to keep the peace, being the people pleaser that I was. Anxiety was also destroying my physical health with the amount of cortisol that was pumping into my system. I was running on empty. I had stomach issues for years, and those eventually led to some complicated health issues I'm still working to heal today.

There are so many layers that I needed to unravel to understand the *why* behind these ways I had been functioning—and this is why it was crucial for me to seek the support of a trusted therapist.

In hindsight, I wish I had known to always trust my gut before my anxiety protector had to come in and set off the alarms. But now, I know that any time I recognize anxiety in my system, it's time to tune in and figure out what it's trying to tell me. (Usually, anxiety comes around when I need to have a conversation that I'm scared to have with someone or when I haven't put boundaries in place and need to. It's still a work in progress.)

Over time, I've learned that it is mandatory that I speak my truth and share my needs. I need to trust that because I'm in alignment with myself, I'm taking care of my own needs so anxiety doesn't need to show up and protect me. Approaching it this way has given me so much emotional freedom to take care of myself and not worry how others may respond to the hard conversations or boundaries I set. It is up to them to take care of their own feelings through their response. I don't need to take that on. It's an amazing feeling to know that anxiety is there if I need her. But I've got it. I'm in control, and she can take a backseat in my system and let me take the wheel.

—Callie

When it comes to anxiety, there are two skills or concepts we want to teach our children:

- Knowing that they are supported through challenges
- Expressing all feelings or fears and accepting help when they are too big to carry alone

For anxiety, the core belief that is being built can vary depending on the situation. However, it can usually be traced back to capacity (versus help-lessness), lovability, or worth.

SKILL: ANXIETY MANAGEMENT

NEGATIVE BELIEF	POSITIVE BELIEF
I am alone	I am not alone
I can't handle this	I am supported
I am not safe	I am safe
I can't get through this	I can get through this
I am helpless	I can get through hard times
I am worthless	I am deserving of love and support

SIGNS OF STRESS AND ANXIETY IN CHILDREN

All children express stress and anxiety symptoms differently. Recognizing signs or patterns of childhood stress can help *you* help your child overcome their feelings of stress. Here are some frequent warning signs of stress in a young child to look out for:

Changes in sleep patterns: If your child has trouble sleeping, has night terrors, or sleeps excessively, it might be an indication of stress or worry.

Mood changes: If your child becomes easily irritated, angry, or unhappy more frequently than normal, they may be showing underlying signs of stress.

Changes in appetite: Stress and anxiety can induce a lack of appetite or overeating. From breakfast to snack time, try observing your child's eating habits to notice any changes in their eating patterns that may indicate stress.

Physical symptoms: Physical symptoms associated with stress and anxiety include headaches, stomach pains, and muscular strain.

Excessive worry: Whether at home or around others in a social setting, if your child appears overly concerned about something, this could be a sign of anxiety.

The Dos of Easing Anxiety in Kids

When it comes to helping your child manage their anxious feelings, there are certain steps you can take—and others you'll want to avoid—when identifying the best approach for supporting them. Here are some things to do:

Promote open communication: Encourage your child to talk about their feelings, thoughts, and experiences to help them feel more supported and less alone.

Build healthy habits together: Planning one-on-one time with your child is a great way to help build a strong connection and find activities you enjoy doing together.

Listen, validate, and identify feelings: Reassure children their feelings are important and that you are there to support them. Consider asking them *why* they feel the way they do to help them lean into their emotions.

Provide a sense of safety and security: Predictability is key to helping children manage stress. Creating a safe and stable home environment with clear rules and routines can help children feel more secure and less anxious.

The Don'ts of Trying to Easing Anxiety in Children

While every situation is different, there are typically some things you'll want to avoid doing, including:

Don't minimize their feelings: It's important to catch yourself before saying things like "Just relax" or "Oh, don't worry about that" to prevent your kids from feeling unsupported when they come to you with a concern.

Don't push them too hard: While encouraging your child to face their fears and overcome their anxiety is important, pushing them too hard can be counterproductive and increase their stress levels.

Don't avoid triggers: Though avoiding uncomfortable circumstances or activities may seem like the easiest solution, doing so can reinforce your anxious child's concerns and make them even more stressed in the long run.

Don't forget self-care: Remember, you can't pour from an empty cup. Be sure to check in with yourself on a daily or weekly basis. And ask for help when you need it.

SEPARATION ANXIETY

Separation anxiety is a normal part of childhood development—but that doesn't always mean it's an easy part for kids or their caregivers to navigate. For some parents, leaving a distressed child in the care of others can come with different levels of discomfort, while others might benefit from having familiar friends or family available to provide care. But no matter your comfort level with separation anxiety, learning about it and how to cope with it may help to ease the process.

For parents of babies (or neurodivergent children), it might not always be possible to communicate verbally that you understand how they feel and reassure them that you'll come back. For children old enough to understand, however, the way you connect with them about their separation anxiety can make a big difference. Instead of trying to talk them out of what they're experiencing, acknowledge that their feelings are valid and show you understand and support them.

For example, you can let them express their feelings. Avoid shushing them or making argumentative statements like "We do this every day" or "There's no reason to be upset." You can also respond with acceptance and calm. Welcome the feelings they express, validate them, and offer simple but truthful reassurances about when you'll return. For instance, you might say, "I hear that you don't want to go. You are safe here with [caregiver's name]. I'll be back after you finish eating dinner."

You're Always Connected, Even When You're Apart

As you journey through the early stages of parenthood, encountering separation anxiety in your child can be both a heart-tugging and a concerning experience. It's important to understand that separation anxiety is a natural, developmental phase, reflective of the deep bond you've nurtured with your child.

Imagine separation anxiety as a testament to the love and trust your child feels in your presence. It's their way of expressing discomfort when apart from their primary source of safety and comfort: you. During these times, your little one might cling closer, cry during farewells, or seem hesitant to engage in previously enjoyed activities like school or playdates.

Navigating this phase with empathy and patience is key. Begin by gradually introducing the concept of separation. Start with brief periods apart and progressively extend them, fostering your child's confidence in your return. Establishing a predictable and affectionate goodbye ritual can also offer reassurance. This could be a special hug or a loving phrase that becomes a comforting routine. Reassure your child of your return, using terms they understand. Consistency in your actions builds trust and security. Introducing a comfort object, like a cherished toy or blanket, can also provide a sense of continuity and comfort in your absence.

Separation anxiety, while challenging, is a phase that most children outgrow. It's an opportunity for you to reinforce their sense of security and independence, gently guiding them toward becoming confident and self-assured individuals. With your understanding, patience, and consistent support, this phase, too, shall pass, leaving behind valuable lessons in emotional resilience for both you and your child.

AFFIRMATION

I can do hard things,
and get through tough days.
I am strong
and supported in so many ways.

During one of our visits to a local hospital, where we were donating Slumberkins to bring comfort to the children there, we encountered a moment that profoundly shifted our perspective and inspired the creation of the Stress Relief (Alpaca) collection. In the quiet corridors of the pediatric wing, we met a young child, anxiously waiting for their treatment. The weight of their anxiety was palpable, not just in their small, tense frame but also in the worried glances exchanged by their parents. Witnessing the child's distress and the parents' feelings of helplessness struck a deep chord in us. It was a heartbreaking realization that sometimes, the hardest battles are fought in the mind, especially for little ones in such intimidating settings.

This encounter sparked a realization: we needed something more than just a comforting toy. We needed a tool that could bridge the gap between children's unspoken anxieties and parents' earnest desire to support them. This led to the birth of the Stress Relief (Alpaca) collection—a thoughtfully designed Slumberkin that could be more than just a soft companion. Alpaca became a medium for crucial conversations about anxiety, offering not just comfort but also a way for parents to navigate through these challenging discussions with their children.

Alpaca, with its calming presence, was designed to be a reassuring friend for children undergoing hospital stays or medical visits, helping them cope with the stress and uncertainty. But its impact didn't stop there. It became evident that Alpaca's gentle support was universal, offering solace in various situations where anxiety might surface. Now, Alpaca is not just a favorite among children in hospitals but a beloved companion in many homes, helping families tackle the complexities of anxiety together.

—Callie and Kelly

Circumstances beyond our control stir up worries and anxieties, creating waves in our otherwise calm emotional waters. In these moments, one effective way to alleviate anxiety is through the practice of consciously passing the worry to someone or something else. This concept is at the heart of why we created our Stress Relief collection.

We wanted to make something tangible that could help "hold worries," by setting up a character that has a captivating story to engage a child's imagination, allowing the space for them to lean into their trust and belief. They are able to let go of their worries, experiencing a sense of relief and unburdening. It's akin to setting down a heavy backpack after a long journey.

WHEN TO SEEK SUPPORT

Recognizing that your child may suffer from anxiety can be a difficult feeling for a parent. It's hard to distinguish between anxiety that is manageable with your help and anxiety that is significant enough to warrant professional help. Consider the following when you're trying to decide to reach out to a therapist.

Intensity and duration: If the signs of anxiety are intense, persistent, and interfere with your child's daily life—such as their ability to attend school, interact with family, or play—it's time to consider seeking help.

Impact on family life: When a child's anxiety starts to significantly impact family routines or relationships, professional support can be beneficial for both the child and the family.

Self-soothing methods fail: If your usual methods of comforting your child or helping them manage their worries aren't effective and the anxiety seems to be escalating, seeking external support is a wise step.

Child's request for help: If your child expresses a desire to talk to someone about their worries or indicates that they are struggling, honor their request by seeking professional guidance.

Parental intuition: Trust your gut. If something feels off, even if you can't pinpoint exactly what it is, consulting a professional can provide clarity and direction.

AFFIRMATION

I am strong and supported.
I am never alone.
Climbing these mountains
will lead me home.

PARENT REFLECTION MOMENT: ANXIETY

Feeling anxiety is part of being human, but as we discussed in this chapter, some situations bring on more stress and anxiety than others. Whether you, your child, or your whole family is struggling with anxiety or stress, you'll likely need lots of moments to check in with yourself.

Here are some questions to consider if you would like to implement our CALM Moment with a focus on Anxiety. You can return to Chapter 5, pages 98–100 ("CALM Moments") to have an outline of this process as you engage in the following Reflection Questions.

In moments of struggle, when seeking clarity and self-comfort, ponder these questions:

- Is this stressor something solvable right now? Or is it something I need to cope with?
- What coping skills and support do I have to get what I need here?
- Does my child need help working through their worry, or do they need help coping with a big worry that can't be solved?

If reflecting on anxiety in general, consider:

- What healthy coping skills do I have to manage stress and anxiety?
- Who can I talk to when I feel worried?

Things to Remember

- Anxiety holds a significant adaptive purpose in our internal systems and our lives.
- Recognizing signs or patterns of childhood stress can help you help your child overcome their feelings of stress.
- Learning how to help a child with separation anxiety starts with understanding its causes and identifying the techniques you can use to encourage resilience.
- Separation anxiety is a natural developmental phase, reflective of the deep bond you've nurtured with your child.

SLUMBERKINS CHARACTER CONNECTION: ALPACA

CHAPTER 18

Grief and Loss

One of the most difficult, unavoidable emotions we face is grief. Grief is a natural emotional response to a loss. If you have loved someone or something deeply, you have also felt an equal measure of grief after you lost it. Loss can be associated with a big change (like moving or not being able to see your friends during a pandemic), or it could be the death of a loved one. All losses can be painful or difficult to experience because humans are built to connect with loved ones and to miss them when they are gone. We enjoy things that are consistent, and thus change can throw us for a loop.

Grief and loss are difficult no matter how or when you experience them, and we all cope with grief in our own ways. There are many children and families all over the world who are experiencing grief and loss now. Some have experienced the death of a loved one or beloved family pet, while others are experiencing the loss of a life they once knew before a big move or a family unit after a divorce. Some families have time to see a loss and prepare, while others are forced into the turmoil of navigating unexpected loss.

Depending on many factors, like your culture, belief systems, and how you were raised, you may have very different beliefs and context about this painful and normal human emotion. Many cultures across the world acknowledge that this is not an emotion that is meant to be held and dealt with alone. Grief can be a very complex emotion that requires connection and support.

THE GRIEF PROCESS

Over the last 20 years, research on the grief process has undergone significant shifts, moving away from rigid models toward a more fluid understanding. Here's an overview of how perspectives have evolved:

From stages to continuums: Earlier models like Kübler-Ross's five stages of grief (denial, anger, bargaining, depression, acceptance) were once widely accepted. However, recent research suggests grief doesn't follow a linear or stage-based progression. Instead, it's now seen as a more dynamic, individualized process in which people might revisit different emotions without a set sequence.

Recognition of continuing bonds: Earlier grief theories often emphasized detachment from the deceased as a goal of healthy mourning. However, more recent studies advocate for the concept of "continuing bonds," where maintaining a connection to the deceased, through memories or symbolic activities, is considered healthy and normal.

Understanding complex grief: The last two decades have seen an increased focus on complications in the grieving process, such as prolonged grief disorder (PGD), previously known as complicated grief. This has led to better understanding and treatment for those who experience intense, enduring grief.

Cultural considerations: There's a growing recognition of the role of cultural, social, and individual factors in shaping the grief experience. Research now emphasizes that grieving practices and expressions are highly influenced by cultural norms and personal circumstances.

Post-traumatic growth: There's an emerging focus on the concept of post-traumatic growth, in which individuals experience personal growth, deeper relationships, and a greater appreciation for life following a loss.

Grief and mental health: Contemporary research increasingly explores the intersection of grief and mental health issues. The relationship between grief and disorders like depression and anxiety is better understood, leading to more integrated therapeutic approaches.

Technology and grief: With the advent of digital technology and social media, recent research has also explored how these platforms are used for expressing grief and memorializing the deceased.

Resilience in grieving: Modern grief research also focuses on resilience and the factors that contribute to healthy adaptation to loss. This perspective acknowledges that while grief is a universal experience, individuals possess varying degrees of resilience and coping mechanisms.

We have seen a significant shift in understanding grief as a highly personal, nonlinear process influenced by a multitude of factors, including cultural and individual differences. This has led to more holistic and person-centered approaches in supporting those who are grieving.

From early on, I heard the family history that my father had been abused and deeply traumatized in his childhood. He tried to work on himself, but he never quite unlocked himself from how trapped he was by his early childhood traumas.

As a child, I couldn't understand why my dad was so inconsistent. How could he be so present and loving one minute, then turn into someone else in the flash of a second? As most children do in this situation, I took on the belief that it was my responsibility to keep things stable in my family by making sure I was a "good girl", putting others needs before my own and achieving accolades to prove my worth. Everything shifted when I had my first son. My father loved my son, and I got to see how he likely was with me when I was a child. Loving, connected, playful. . . but at times, unpredictable and mean. I had slowly been trying to engage with my father in conversations, stating my needs and opinions about behavior around me and my children. Most of these were brushed off and not taken seriously. Everything came to a head after my son's third birthday that my father (after drinking as usual) was particularly unkind. It was nothing unusual for him, but it was the last straw for me. I set a hard boundary (also not in the most kind way), which happened between us sometimes. But it was different this time. I was no longer going to expose my child (or my own inner child) to unpredictable and hurtful treatment from anyone anymore, even if that person was my father. After our fight, we didn't talk for years.

Going through this experience has been a journey filled with grief for me, my mother, my brother, and my children (especially my oldest) who had three years of connection with his grandfather. Dealing with an estrangement is never easy, and it's especially hard to explain to a three and five-year-old. Their grandfather is alive, he lives down the road, and we don't see him.

I lean heavily into the concept of Heart Family with my children when explaining why we can't see "Moo-Pa" anymore. I tell my boys that families change and no matter what, feeling safe and loved is essential in any relationship. Even if it's your parent, best friend, or partner, if they stop treating you with respect and hurt you, you can change the boundaries of the relationship.

—Kelly

When supporting grief and loss, there are two concepts we want children to understand:

- Loss and having to say goodbye to things and people we love is a natural part of life.
- All emotions are welcome and the memories of loved ones will remain in their hearts.

For grief and loss, the core beliefs that are being built are connected to our experience of connection, disconnection and our capacity to handle the unknown.

SKILL: GRIEF & LOSS

NEGATIVE BELIEF	POSITIVE BELIEF
I will never get through this	I can get through this
I am alone	I'm never alone
It is my fault	It's not my fault
I have to hide my feelings/ I need to be past these feelings	All my feelings are welcome

Grief is the other side of the coin to attachment or love. If we have experienced a deep love for someone, then it is inevitable that we will feel grief when that love is "lost." What we have heard from others and experienced ourselves through grieving, however, is that love is actually never lost. It is through our continued and changing relationship to the love we felt from and for that person (essentially our grief) that we continue to benefit and keep loving despite that person being gone in physical form.

—Kelly

PROACTIVELY INTRODUCING THE CONCEPT OF GOODBYES

We understand it can feel overwhelming to try to explain such complex concepts to your child, especially if you, like so many of us, feel uncomfortable thinking about and talking about death or loss.

It can be tough to get ourselves to proactively lean in to hard topics when we're already dealing with so many other things in our parenting lives. When it comes to grief and loss, there is a way to begin introducing the concept of hellos and goodbyes so that kids can learn about all types of goodbyes that may involve feelings of grief and loss, not just about death. Supporting this learning in a pre-emptive and supportive way may not protect from the feelings of pain or grief when we experience loss, but it does help lay the conceptual groundwork to help a child understand what is happening in the moment.

This may seem a little fluffy to include here in this section, but in a child's world of understanding the concept of loss, it's an important piece to highlight, especially if we are looking to proactively support and build a foundation of emotional health and wellness for our children. We naturally want to push pain away, but we are here to support the welcoming of *all* feelings, because at the end of the day, we will all experience loss and the heaviness of grief in our lives. When we are supporting our own feelings and emotions in the aftermath of a loss, it can be very difficult to figure out how we can show up for our children at the same time.

Kids form attachments to many things as they are developing. Sometimes that can be a favorite toy or even a pair of shoes. They are growing and changing so quickly that many times, items will represent a feeling or a time that was meaningful, comforting, or important to them. This is a great inroad to talking about how time moves and we say goodbye to some things, but the cycle constantly changes.

Our brains naturally want to find stability and comfort but are constantly being thrown into change and growth. Through that process, we must learn to say goodbye so that we can turn our heads and look for the hello to come. We can find small moments of this in our children's lives as they grow. They often bring us to tears! When they don't wear that cute onesie anymore and now they are in size 4! Even the process of growing up brings up feelings of grief for these special fleeting moments with our children. If we can help our kids know that all of those feelings are part of what makes them human and that all of that is beautiful, we are setting them up to understand these concepts as they grow.

AFFIRMATION

I can say goodbye.
I can say hello.
My memories and
love will never go.

WHEN YOU'VE LOST A LOVED ONE

We know that everything may feel upside down for you and your family at this time. We understand that your family has experienced the death of someone close to you and know that grief cannot be turned off at times when school, work, or parenting demands may arise.

The grief process looks different for everyone.

10 FACTS ABOUT CHILDREN AND GRIEF

Here are some facts about children and grief that you may not know.

Fact 1: No Two Grief Experiences Are the Same   There is no right way to grieve. Everyone grieves in their own way, even within the same family.

Fact 2: Grief Is Cyclical   Children do not move through concrete "stages" of emotional experiences but rather cycle through a spectrum of emotions and thoughts about their loss multiple times each day/week/year.

The "Tasks of Grieving Children" on the following chart outlines details on supporting children through these cycles.

TASKS OF GRIEVING CHILDREN

The Dougy Center for Grieving Children and Families outlines three "Tasks of Grieving Children and Teens," drawing from decades of observation supporting children and families in grief groups and work from grief experts Worden and Wolfelt.

FIRST TASK: To understand that the person is dead.

This is a thinking process in which children need to understand the facts. Their curiosity is a healthy part of the process as they attempt to grasp the meaning of what has occurred.

Adults can help by:

- Providing direct and honest information.
- Using correct language instead of euphemisms (i.e., "dead" instead of "passed away").
- Including children in the process and offering them choices about how much to be involved.
- Answering questions as many times as needed (repetition helps).
- Allowing children to observe the grief process of the adults in their lives while not becoming a caregiver for those adults.

SECOND TASK: To feel the emotions about the death.

This is a feeling process in which grief feels physical and is reflected in the body sensations (sleeplessness, tearfulness, appetite changes) that can propel behaviors (acting out, overachieving, withdrawing).

Adults can help by:

- Encouraging safe, physical outlets such as active play, movement, and creativity.
- Reflecting the child's process through play and language, rather than asking direct questions.
- Listening, caring about, and accepting the child's unique expressions of grief.
- Reassuring the child they are not alone, and that feelings of guilt are common.
- Lowering expectations while they are moving through the immense and energy-intensive process of grief.

THIRD TASK: To go on living and loving after the person has died.

This process involves children and adults understanding the death as a part of the ongoing story of who they are while they continue to go on living. The person who died is still a part of their memories as they begin to ask, "What can I do now?"

Adults can help by:

- Celebrating the grief journey and the steps taken toward reconciliation of tasks.
- Trusting in the unique grief process of the child and family.
- Allowing for pauses from grief for relaxation and fun.

Fact 3: Grief Is a Dual Process   It is essential that children and adults understand that a person in grief can and will also experience joy. The oscillation between emotions that prompt us to reach out to others, and those that invite us into solitude, is normal. Moments of respite from intense emotions can often be accompanied by feelings of guilt for taking a "time out" from grief.

Fact 4: Play Is the Language of Grief for Children   Children may enact their experience using you as a stand-in for people in their lives.

Fact 5: Grief Cannot Be "Fixed"   We can demonstrate trust in the child's ability to journey through their grief process by creating a safe, child-led outlet for them to express themselves without an expectation of "taking away their pain."

Fact 6: There Is No "Right" Thing to Say   Lead with honesty, admit when there's something you don't know ("Where do we go after we die?"), and be present to help support your child through their emotional processing.

Fact 7: Connection with a Supportive Adult Can Make a Huge Difference   The aftermath of a loss can significantly impact how children perceive their experience for years to come.

Fact 8: There Is No "End" to Grief   Children will re-grieve throughout their lives as they move through different developmental stages and can understand their loss in new ways. It can feel messy and incomplete. That is OK!

Fact 9: Complicated Grief Does Happen   Indications that grief is complex include prolonged symptoms that impact a child's functioning. Remember, additional support is available. The Dougy Center (www.dougy.org) provides a national search feature to find grief support groups in your area.

Fact 10: Start with You! Grief will touch all of us throughout our lives. The very fact that the experience is universal means we must pause to consider the following: just because I've grieved does not mean I "understand" others' unique experiences.

HOW TO TALK TO A CHILD ABOUT DEATH

There's no one-size-fits-all rule when it comes to discussing a sensitive subject like death with a child. Talking about it can be challenging for adults because our comfort level tells us to avoid difficult conversation topics if we don't have all of the right answers. However, feel empowered to tackle the subject around children and grief directly if your child asks you a question about death or if there's been a significant loss in the family.

When it's time to discuss the topic, consider the following ways to express ideas they can grasp and make sense of:

Use simple sentences: Formulate answers that your child can comprehend by keeping your responses simple and using vocabulary they understand.

Be honest: Rather than sugar-coating your words, be as honest as possible. If you're telling them that their pet has died, try to avoid vague answers like "They're no longer with us" or "They passed away." Most children don't understand euphemisms, so the truth is much easier for them to comprehend.

Respond concretely: Instead of giving generalities, try to use concrete information when explaining death. Answer your child's question with a concrete response like "She had a sickness called leukemia and the medicine couldn't help her get better."

LESSON IN SUPPORTING SOMEONE THROUGH GRIEF

While we have both experienced forms of grief for various reasons, we asked our friend and co-worker (the first employee at Slumberkins, actually) to share her story.

Our oldest child, Ella, was about a year and a half when we found out we were having a second child. We were thrilled, and I had a totally normal, very healthy pregnancy.

My son Ethan was born at full term on a Friday; he was healthy and happy. When we took him home from the hospital on Saturday, he started having some trouble eating, and as the evening went on, we started noticing a little rasp in his breathing. By Sunday morning, we brought him to the ER to figure out what was causing these issues.

Doctors brought Ethan to the NICU and spent Sunday and Monday monitoring and running tests. On Monday evening, our team of doctors told us that Ethan had an extremely rare genetic disorder, and he was not going to get better. We ultimately made the heart-wrenching decision to let Ethan die in our arms rather than risk being told that he died on an operating table during a procedure that would not provide him with a meaningful quality of life.

Everything happened so fast that I was functioning in a state of heartbreak and shock. Confronting the reality of what just happened to us and Ethan, while still needing to care for Ella, was a paradox of feelings I wouldn't wish on any parent.

We picked up Ella from daycare after leaving the hospital and told her the two-year-old version of what happened:

"Ethan died. His body didn't work properly, and he is not going to come home and live with us."

She said, "OK," and was ready to go play with her toys.

My husband and I both lost our child and needed to care for our own grief, but we still had a two-year-old daughter at home who needed her mom and dad. We had agreed that we wanted Ella's life to stay as similar as possible to how it was before Ethan died. We still talked about Ethan and let her see that we were sad or tired or whatever was honest, but only so much as we could do so while ensuring that her needs were being prioritized. If we couldn't meet her needs and help her take care of her feelings, we would excuse ourselves and ask for help. If help was not available, we took care of her together to lean on each other.

I am so thankful that in Ella's world, what happened was not immediately traumatic to her. Her reality was not shaken by the fact that her brother didn't live very long after he was born. It's been one of the hardest and most heartwarming things to watch Ella grow up over the last five years with Ethan as a part of her life. She's asked more questions about him and why he doesn't live with us, why he died, as she's gotten older and seen her friends welcome new siblings, and we've prioritized giving her honest, age-appropriate responses:

"He was really sick. Your body is safe and healthy, and his was sick and didn't work properly. He died, and he's not going to come back, but we will remember him."

If you're going through grief right now, make sure to take care of your needs first. You can't take care of your family if you're not taking care of yourself. And if you can't take care of yourself, enlist the help of someone else to take care of you.

—Alissa

As Alissa experienced, the first rule of thumb is that grief looks different and it includes all emotions. People used to think that grief was a linear process—something you move through and come out the other side. That theory has been completely disproven. Grief does not exclude joy. You can be sad about what happened but still find reasons to laugh. Alissa told us that people were surprised to see her and her husband laughing so soon after Ethan's death, but that makes complete sense to us.

Grief is more like a relationship that you grow with over time; the amount of love and connection that you have felt with the person who is no longer with you changes, moves, evolves over time. In some ways, it can be just as complex as when they were here. Grief doesn't really have an expiration date. It's not "over" at any certain point.

Moving through grief while still parenting can feel impossible.

Managing boundaries and communication was hugely important for Alissa. It can feel hard and overwhelming, but asking people directly to show up in the way that you need them to is hugely beneficial . . . for you and for them.

IF YOUR CHILD IS STRUGGLING WITH GRIEF/LOSS

Death is a natural part of life, yet many of us adults may not have been taught how to cope with or process grief, much less how to talk to kids about death. Helping our children learn strategies for dealing with loss can be both healing and rewarding. It can also be plenty of worrying: what if we say the wrong thing?

While it may be tempting to put on a brave face and act like you're fine, showing your child your feelings of sadness or dismay helps them understand that it's OK to feel these feelings. Expressing your own emotions is a great healthy parenting habit and modeling physical closeness through snuggling or hugging is another good way to provide reassurance.

Rest assured that your time, care, and attention go an incredibly long way for your child during this process. Be honest, have faith in yourself, and try these tips for supporting your child through grief.

Self-care: Parents are probably getting sick of hearing this, but it is so vital to take care of your own needs and feelings first. Children are wired to connect with their parents, and they sense the emotional states of the adults and peers around them.

Understand behaviors: All behavior is communication. Children will often show their grief through testing boundaries or acting out (and sometimes withdrawing). Grief for kids can often look like defiant or acting-out behaviors. Your child also may act like a younger version of themselves, becoming clingy or needy.

Talk about it: Children will sense changes in the family and can often believe these changes are their fault. We recommend that you talk to your children about the loss, even if you aren't sure they will understand. Choose developmentally appropriate language.

Be consistent: In the midst of changes, children need reassurance. We recommend trying hard to stick to a regular routine and schedule. Posting a visual schedule (a schedule with words and pictures for each step) can be helpful for children to feel more confident about what comes next in their day.

Play: Children process and express feelings through play. Allow plenty of time for your child to play on their own, and with you.

Food, water, exercise, sleep: Grief and loss show up in our bodies. Our bodies help us to communicate our feelings and process them. It's always good to take care of our bodies, but we need to do so even more when we are experiencing grief.

Get more support: Some types of grief and loss are typical, and others can be scary or traumatic. Check with a mental health provider or medical provider to explore your options for additional support in your community.

AFFIRMATION

Though today is hard,
I am going to start
The journey ahead
with you in my heart.

PARENT REFLECTION MOMENT: GRIEF AND LOSS

When our children are struggling with grief and loss, oftentimes we are too. It's so important to make sure we are taking care of ourselves and checking in with what support we need too. Proactively exploring themes of grief and loss can also be helpful to make sure we are staying open to the range of human emotions.

Here are some questions to consider if you would like to implement our CALM Moment with a focus on Grief and Loss. You can return to Chapter 5, pages 98–100 ("CALM Moments") to have an outline of this process as you engage in the following Reflection Questions:

In moments of struggle, when seeking clarity and self-comfort, ponder these questions:

- Assess your basic needs: Do you need to eat, sleep, or drink water? Remember, caring for your physical well-being is crucial during times of grief.

- Consider the kind of support or people you need around you to navigate through this challenging period.

For broader contemplation on grief and loss:

- Reflect on your early learnings about feelings, goodbyes, and loss. How have these influenced your understanding of grief?
- Think about the losses you've experienced in your life and how they have shaped you.
- Explore ways to normalize and accommodate grief and loss in your home, creating a space where these feelings can be expressed and processed.

Things to Remember

- Grief looks different for everyone. The process is nonlinear and doesn't have an "end."
- Be honest with your children about loss and use concrete words to help them understand.
- Join forces with teachers and coaches to create a plan to support your child when they're away from you.

SLUMBERKINS CHARACTER CONNECTION: SPRITE

CHAPTER 19

Self-Expression

It can be so easy to tell other people when to stand up for themselves . . . and so hard to do it yourself. As educators, we've worked with many students who struggled with the ability to speak up for themselves. Many of the interventions and supports we provided and taught helped them learn how to advocate for themselves by asking for what they need. Just by being honest with ourselves, and with others, we can be our own best advocate.

EXPRESSING YOUR NEEDS

Can you think of a time when you kept your thoughts and opinions to yourself to keep the peace because you knew that if you expressed your feelings there might be a giant fight? And then if the situation goes south, you kick yourself for not speaking up? Maybe this happens daily because you're trying to appease a family member or a partner. Perhaps it has escalated so sharply that you don't even know how to begin to start expressing your feelings, especially because you suspect those feelings won't be welcomed or valued. Eventually, your self-esteem takes a big hit, and you are no longer able to advocate for yourself.

If we are being honest, we've both been in relationships in which we didn't follow our own advice. We valued peace in the moment rather than peace within ourselves, even though we know that abandoning our needs rarely yields positive results.

We should have trusted our innate ability to tune in to ourselves and follow our inner wisdom (gut feelings). Trusting that wisdom, staying aligned with our feelings, and communicating those feelings with others are skills that weren't necessarily taught to us as kids. We grew up in the people-pleasing era; if you did happen to be a person who spoke their mind, you might have been pigeonholed as a "troublemaker" or "difficult."

We now live in the boundary-setting era; we're starting to put our own needs first by creating boundaries with our kids, partners, families, and friends because we know that doing so is a vital part of our emotional health. We want to make sure you and your child have those skills, too.

Setting boundaries (which are the lines we draw to establish our comfort and preferences in relationships with others) takes practice, and it's not always easy to do. But once you begin carving out space for yourself, you'll feel the relief and the freedom of expressing your needs. Whether or not your relationship partner accommodates those needs, you'll still feel the benefits of honoring yourself and your own needs. Having that first conversation can feel intimidating, and you may need to retrain your nervous system to be ready for any sort of response you'll receive, but it will be worth it in the end.

The best part about improving your own ability to express yourself is that you can set your kids up for success without them fighting the battles you've fought. With the knowledge you've learned, you can teach them to hack the emotional development system.

Let's dive into a real-life example of this.

It's hard for me to admit that there was a time in the not-so-distant past when I was living my life as an unconscious people-pleasing monster. I couldn't set a boundary and deal with the aftermath to save my life.

There's nothing like parenting to wake up the boundary-setting giant that sleeps in all of us as mothers. Some people may turn into a "mama bear," but when I first stumbled into figuring out how to set boundaries, I was more like Te Kā, the fiery goddess in "Moana."

As I bumbled my way through trying to express my feelings and set boundaries for my kids, I discovered that there is a skill and a practice to implement along the way. The biggest piece of the puzzle for me was doing the self-work to really tune in to myself without the noise of outside influences or opinions. I really needed to find that inner wisdom, those gut instincts I hadn't listened to for years.

I also had to do a lot of practice in an emotionally safe relationship. For me, that was my friendship with Kelly. As co-founders and co-CEOs of Slumberkins, we are basically in a platonic marriage. Through my interactions with Kelly, I honed the ability to speak up, lead, be okay with conflict, and hold space for my feelings as the business grew and evolved. Eventually, I became braver about speaking up in all aspects of my life.

—Callie

When we think about the skills that make up healthy self-expression, there are two concepts we want to teach children:

- How to tune in to themselves to be able to identify how they are feeling
- How to express that feeling or need (setting a boundary)

For self-expression, the core belief that is being built is the concept of self-worth.

SKILL: SELF-EXPRESSION

NEGATIVE BELIEF	POSITIVE BELIEF
My feelings don't matter	My feelings are valid
I can't trust myself	I can trust myself
My body is not mine	My body is my own
I am helpless	I am strong
I can't use my voice	I can speak up for myself
Setting boundaries is not OK (or is mean)	Setting boundaries is OK (and it shows people how I want to be treated)

PROACTIVELY BUILDING SELF-EXPRESSION SKILLS

Tuning in to ourselves, communicating our feelings and needs, and setting boundaries are absolutely vital for our emotional health and well-being. You see, when we really listen to our inner voice and honor our true feelings, we're not just being authentic, we're also nurturing our mental and emotional health. It's like having a heartfelt conversation with yourself in which you acknowledge and validate your own experiences. We need to seek and build honest and healthy relationships so we will feel safe expressing our feelings and needs to others; doing so will create a space in which we can be our true selves without fear.

Setting boundaries is crucial to our relationships. It's like drawing a personal map that defines where we end and others begin, ensuring we don't lose ourselves in the chaos of daily life. This isn't just self-care; it's a deep, respectful nod to our own worth and dignity. It's about saying "I value myself enough to recognize what I need and speak up so I can get it." Each step we take in understanding and expressing ourselves is a step toward a more authentic and fulfilling life.

As adults, we can use our logical mind and inner voice to decide which boundaries are non-negotiable, but children have to learn this skill. We know that a child's inner voice is in it's foundational formational years until about the age of seven, so helping a child tune in to themselves and cultivate the practice of finding their inner voice is a valuable part of their emotional and psychological development. You may remember that in Chapter 3, "Expanding on Core Beliefs," we gave general guidance for helping children develop an encouraging inner voice.

Now, we're going to help you guide your child as they use that inner voice to express themselves and make decisions:

Encourage reflection and self-questioning: Foster an environment in which the child feels comfortable reflecting on their experiences and feelings. Encourage them to ask themselves questions like "How do I feel about this?" or "What do I really want or need in this situation?" This doesn't need to be a dramatic stop-the-presses conversation. These can be casual questions on the way home from basketball practice to help them become more aware of their inner thoughts and feelings, and gradually, they'll start recognizing their own voice.

Provide opportunities for choice: Give the child opportunities to make choices, starting with simple decisions like picking out clothes or choosing a book to read. Respect their choices (even if you would have chosen differently) and encourage them to think about why they made those decisions. This empowers them to trust their judgment and understand that their opinions and preferences matter.

Promote journaling or expressive activities: Encourage activities like journaling, drawing, or storytelling, which allow the child to express themselves freely. These activities can be powerful tools for children to explore their thoughts and feelings, helping them to articulate and understand their inner voice.

Practice active listening: When the child speaks, listen attentively and without judgment (or cell phones). Validate their feelings and thoughts, and avoid immediately offering solutions or opinions. This shows that their voice is valued and respected, reinforcing their confidence to express themselves and listen to their inner guidance.

Remember, the goal is to help your child feel secure and valued in their self-expression. Once they know they can trust you with their thoughts and feelings, they will share even more. Your active and empathetic listening will become a wonderful model for what they deserve in future relationships, and over time, they'll develop the ability to tune in to their inner voice.

AFFIRMATION

I can say what I need.
I know I belong.
I speak my truth when I feel it.
I am worthy and strong.

IF YOUR CHILD IS STRUGGLING WITH SELF-EXPRESSION

In addition to building your child's ability to listen to their inner voice, you should also be on the lookout for signs that they might not be expressing their true feelings or setting boundaries that will help them grow in the emotional and social realms. Here are some key indicators to watch out for:

Difficulty saying "no" or expressing discomfort: If your child consistently seems unable or unwilling to say "no" to requests or demands from others, even when they are clearly uncomfortable, it may indicate a struggle with boundary setting. They might also have a hard time expressing their needs or desires, often deferring to what others want.

Withdrawal or excessive shyness: Children who are overly withdrawn or shy, especially in social situations in which they previously felt comfortable, might be experiencing challenges with self-expression. This can manifest as reluctance to speak up, share opinions, or participate in group activities.

Overly agreeable behavior: If your child always seems to agree with others, even when it goes against their personal interests or beliefs, this might be a sign that they are struggling to assert their own views and set boundaries.

Physical signs of discomfort in social situations: Watch for physical cues like fidgeting, lack of eye contact, or physical withdrawal in social interactions. These can be signs of discomfort with expressing themselves or setting boundaries.

Frustration or resentment in relationships: If your child frequently expresses frustration or resentment in their interactions with friends or family members, it could be due to a lack of skills in expressing their needs and setting healthy boundaries.

Imitating others excessively: While it's normal for children to imitate peers as a way of learning, over-reliance on copying others can indicate a lack of confidence in their own choices.

Difficulty making decisions: Hesitation or distress over making decisions, even simple ones, can be a sign that a child is not in tune with their own preferences and may need support in understanding and expressing their own desires.

Changes in behavior or mood: Becoming easily upset, angry, or tearful can sometimes be linked to struggles with self-expression and boundary setting.

One day I received a voicemail from the school counselor at my daughter's school. She had been doing a small group lesson on setting boundaries and wanted to fill me in on a sensitive topic that came up with Cora when she was six years old.

When Cora came home, she definitely acted shy about talking to me. After some gentle questioning, she finally admitted to me that she did not want to be tickled when she was being woken up in the morning. We have a live-in au pair and sometimes when she was trying to wake Cora up for school, she would just gently tickle her.

The next step was for Cora to communicate this with our au pair. She was extremely reluctant to have the conversation and said she needed my support. So we cuddled up together and re-read the book *Lynx Sets Boundaries* as a refresher and reminder that it is completely normal to set boundaries and express our feelings to others.

Together, we went and had the conversation with our au pair. I had to support Cora through most of the talking, and when we shared what was making Cora uncomfortable, our au pair completely understood and was very sweet and kind throughout the conversation. She asked Cora how she would like to be woken up and made a plan for the morning routine. (Sometimes Cora does not want to get up as early as she needs to on school days.)

It's been about a year since that conversation and I am so proud of Cora for gaining skills in this area. I often hear her say to me or her brothers, "I don't like that," "That makes me feel weird," "I need some space," or, "No thanks, I don't want to do that." All of these phrases tell me that she's standing up for herself and communicating it to others.

—Callie

SETTING BOUNDARIES

In the previous example, we discussed setting physical boundaries. But there are other boundaries kids should be aware of, like emotional and verbal boundaries. Helping kids understand and set healthy boundaries is absolutely crucial for their development, safety, and well-being. In addition to building their self-advocacy skills, setting boundaries improves their comfort levels. Here are two options to help you teach this important skill:

Use simple, relatable scenarios: You can discuss personal space using the idea of an "invisible bubble" around each person. This bubble represents their comfort zone. Teach children that just as they have their own bubble that they don't want others to intrude upon without permission, they should also respect others' bubbles. You can create role-playing games where children practice asking for permission to enter someone's space or saying "no" when they feel uncomfortable.

Teach the "Stop, Think, Choose" method: Equip children with a straightforward decision-making process when it comes to setting boundaries. "Stop, Think, Choose" can be a helpful mantra. First, they stop and recognize a situation in which a boundary might be needed. Next, they think about how the situation makes them feel and what boundary would be appropriate (e.g. saying no to unwanted physical contact, choosing not to share personal information, etc.). Finally, they choose and assertively communicate their boundaries. Reinforce that it's OK to say no in situations where they feel uncomfortable, and it's important to communicate their feelings respectfully and clearly.

In both methods, it's essential to provide a supportive environment where children feel comfortable discussing their feelings and experiences. Regular conversations about boundaries can help children understand and respect their own limits and those of others.

Why Setting Boundaries Is Important for Abuse Prevention

Research shows deeply troubling statistics on child abuse indicating that the abuser is often someone the child knows and trusts: parents, family members, caregivers, or family acquaintances. In cases of sexual abuse, it's particularly common for the abuser to be someone within the child's immediate social circle. This can complicate the child's ability to disclose the abuse, as it might involve someone they have a close relationship with or someone their family trusts.

Understanding and establishing healthy boundaries is a crucial method of preventing abuse. Empowering children with knowledge about boundaries and self-expression helps them recognize and communicate their personal limits and also instill a strong sense of self-worth. It's our hope that being more up front with these key skills can help keep your child safe.

Help Kids to Know Their Boundaries Through Practicing These Tips at Home

Physical Boundaries with Grown-Ups

Gentle pushback for unwanted hugs/kisses: Imagine your little one feeling unsure about a relative insisting on a hug. Teach them to say, "I'd rather not hug right now, but how about a cool secret handshake instead?" This approach is friendly and offers a fun, comfortable alternative.

Personal space reminder: If someone is too close, your child can say, "I like a little more wiggle room, please!" It's a lighthearted way to communicate their need for personal space.

Physical Boundaries with Friends

When sharing toys: When a friend takes your child's toy without asking, they can say, "Can you ask me first next time you want to play with my toys?" It's a polite, clear way to set boundaries around their belongings.

When play gets too rough: If your child is uncomfortable with rough play, they might say, "Let's switch to a game where everyone feels safe, like tag or hide-and-seek!" This not only expresses their discomfort but also suggests a positive alternative.

Emotional Boundaries

With grown-ups: If your child isn't ready to talk about something, encourage them to say, "Can we chat about this later? I need some time to think." It teaches them it's OK to take time to process their emotions.

With friends: If a conversation makes them uncomfortable, your child can try saying, "I don't really want to talk about that. Let's talk about [another topic] instead!" This guides them to steer away from conversations they're not comfortable with.

Tips for Parents

- **Be a role model:** Show them how you use polite and friendly ways to set your own boundaries.
- **Practice makes perfect:** Have fun role-playing these scenarios at home. It can be a game where you both take turns setting boundaries.
- **Cheer them on:** Always let them know how proud you are when they express their needs and boundaries.
- **Talk about different situations:** Share stories or create little scenarios about times they might need to set boundaries—like at a birthday party or during playtime.

Easy Phrases for Little Ones

- "Can we play something we both like?"
- "I'm not OK with that. Let's try this instead."

- "My body, my rules!"
- "I need a moment, please."

Remember, empowering our little ones with these tools is like giving them a superpower—the power to understand and communicate their boundaries. It's all about making it simple, approachable, and a bit fun. This way, they learn the importance of personal space and emotional well-being in the most nurturing way possible.

AFFIRMATION

My body is mine,
I know what I like.
I check in with myself
and say what feels right.

PARENT REFLECTION MOMENT: SELF-EXPRESSION

The topic of self-expression can bring up lots of triggers for parents. You may need to advocate for yourself or your child. By contrast, your child may be a pro at speaking up, and the nonstop dialogue may feel overwhelming.

Checking in with your own reactions is vital to moving through the process with kindness, confidence, and resilience.

Here are some questions to consider if you would like to implement our CALM Moment with a focus on Self-Expression. You can return to Chapter 5, pages 98–100 ("CALM Moments") to have an outline of this process as you engage in the following Reflection Questions.

In moments of struggle, when seeking clarity and self-comfort, ponder these questions:

- Are my child's strong advocacy skills and self-expression skills triggering for me? If so, why?
- What behaviors do I really need to set limits around? What behaviors do I need to allow space for? How can I find a balance here?
- How can I find the inner strength to be myself and express myself clearly for my own behalf or for my child?

For broader reflection on self-expression and setting boundaries, ponder these points:

- How do I feel when I need to set boundaries?
- What did I learn about boundaries in my own family of origin?
- What boundaries do I need to be better about setting? How can I find the inner strength to do so?
- What will I say when I want to set boundaries?

Things to Remember

- It is essential to teach your child to establish boundaries for their physical safety and emotional development.
- Help your child practice deciding on their boundaries and communicating those boundaries to others at home.

- Empower your child with the knowledge that they know themselves best and they can (and should!) ask for what they need.
- Be sure to check in with your child from time to time to see if their preferences or boundaries have shifted.

SLUMBERKINS CHARACTER CONNECTION: LYNX

CHAPTER 20

Creativity

When you think of creativity, you might think of art, music, or using imagination. In some ways, creativity seems like "child's play" because when you witness someone in the flow of creativity, they make it look "easy." In fact, creativity is a complex and multifaceted concept, encompassing the ability to generate new ideas, solutions, or expressions that are both unique and valuable.

Creative people can produce ideas that are original, or "outside the box," and many times those ideas are innovative, solving problems in novel ways. As opposed to finding just one answer to a question, creative people are divergent thinkers and have the capacity to generate multiple solutions to a problem. They can visualize all sorts of new possibilities or scenarios and can adapt easily because they accept that making mistakes is part of the process.

While creativity includes the act of creating art, there's so much more to creativity than we might at first think. Creativity is a form of connection to Self that is so important to stay aware of and connected to. As parents, we can teach our kids that creativity is a way of moving through the world that we bring with us everywhere we go.

What I saw in my work with children was that their access to creativity was integral in supporting their emotional processing and resiliency through difficult moments. Creativity didn't seem to be something to aspire to; rather, it was something that was innately inside everyone in different and unique ways that were supportive to their overall well-being and alignment with their authentic selves.

There seemed to be a narrative that only some people were creative and some of the theories that I started seeing supported that line of thinking. We want to help shift that narrative and help kids and families find inspiration in whatever creative expressions or outlets called to them. We believe in everyone's capacity to tune into creativity as a skill that could be not only a vehicle for expression, but also a tool to create and solve unique issues and problems. I want everyone to know that they have access to this amazing tool that can support their inner world so much.

I believe that creativity comes to us when we need it most. If we are open to letting it guide us through difficult moments and come through us and be open and confident enough to do that, it can really super-charge our purpose and healing throughout our life journey.

This is why we created Dragon for the resilience collection. Don't tell anyone, but it's my favorite character, and I actually even have a large Dragon tattoo. This experience inspired me to tap into my own creative callings and start writing, drawing, and creating worlds to capture these important healing tools for myself and others. Dragon has helped me create Slumberkins.

—Kelly

SUPPORTING CREATIVITY

When thinking about supporting creativity in our child's lives, there are two skills or concepts we want to teach our children:

- They have a unique and valuable perspective that is fun to express and share with others.
- When we tune into ourselves, there is unique creativity in all of us.

For creativity, the core beliefs that are being built can vary depending on the situation. However, it can usually be traced back to resilience, self-acceptance, and authenticity.

SKILL: CREATIVITY

NEGATIVE BELIEF	POSITIVE BELIEF
I am not creative	I am creative
My ideas are not valuable	My ideas are valuable
I must do things the right way	There is no one way to do things
It's not OK to be different	I am unique and I love that
Making mistakes is bad	There are no mistakes, only learning
I am not good enough	I am enough as I am
I can't do anything	My world is what I make it

CREATIVITY THROUGH THE YEARS

We can support and foster creativity in our children, no matter their age. While our approach may vary based on their developmental stage, we can meet our kids where they are and support their sense of safety and freedom.

Babies have not yet developed abstract thought or the ability to engage in pretend games, but their curiosity and interest in exploring the world and their ability to find new uses for objects is a precursor and vital step for other types of creativity later.

Provide a warm, loving, and responsive environment for your little one. This foundation of trust enables infants to feel secure in exploring their world. Engage infants in sensory play activities like playing with soft toys, listening to lullabies, or exploring textures. React positively to their babbling and facial expressions. Mimicking their sounds and expressions encourages communication and emotional expression.

Allow little kids to explore their environment. This can be through unstructured play, using safe household items, or playing in a sandbox. Introduce them to crayons, finger paints, and clay. Don't focus on the end product; rather, celebrate their process and effort. Read to them regularly and encourage them to tell their own stories, even if it's just a few words or gestures. This fosters imagination and narrative skills. You might want to have a dress-up trunk to encourage them to act out their own scenes.

Big kids have the potential to really dive into creativity in their own unique ways through art, play, science, music, dance, fashion, sports, language—you name it. Older kids often struggle with comparing themselves to others, and this can sometimes make for a "creativity block" of sorts. Sometimes, older kids think creativity means just being "good at art," but we can help them tap into a growth mindset when we teach them to explore their unique gifts and strengths and see them as creative forces.

Across all stages, the key is to provide support and encouragement without imposing excessive expectations or judgments. Celebrate their creative endeavors, offer positive feedback, and always be ready to participate or facilitate their creative journey. Remember, each child is unique, and their creativity will manifest in different ways. Being attentive to their individuality and responding to their developmental needs at each stage is crucial in nurturing a lifelong creative.

TIME TO PLAY

When we dive into the realm of creativity, especially through the eyes of our children, it's like stepping into a world where magic and wonder come to life. Creativity is this incredible, sparkling river that flows through each of us, especially our little ones. It's far more than just crayons on paper or building blocks in a tower. Creativity is the language of imagination, the whispers of "what if," and the dance of original, unbound thoughts that each child brings into the world.

Picture your child staring at a cloud and seeing a dragon while all you see is a fluffy cotton ball. That's creativity in its purest form. It's the ability to look at the world and paint it with the colors of their imagination, to see possibilities where others see the ordinary. It's the stories kids tell with their toys, each character coming to life with a personality and an adventure all its own.

Creativity is also the courage to explore, to ask questions, and to express themselves in unique ways. It's in the songs they hum spontaneously, the forts they build from pillows, and the make-believe worlds in which they are the heroes, the explorers, or the caretakers of magical creatures. This isn't just play; it's their creative minds weaving tapestries of ideas and emotions.

But creativity isn't only about what they create; it's also about how they feel and connect. When children express themselves, they are sharing a piece of their inner world. Whether it's through a painted picture, a story, or a dance, they are opening a window to their emotions and thoughts, making sense of their experiences in their unique, creative way.

As parents, when we encourage and embrace this creative spirit, we're not just inspiring them to make something; we're empowering them to think, feel, and express themselves in ways that only they can. And in doing so, we're helping them build the foundations of a joyful, vibrant, and imaginative life.

To your young child, the world provides endless opportunities to create. Through imaginative play—often saturated in slaying dragons, playing house, and capturing villains—children can learn about the world around them and cultivate their creative thinking skills.

That said, the benefits of pretend play sessions swirling in make-believe monsters and heroic swashbucklers extend beyond the playroom. Imaginative play can also help build self-confidence and encourage social interaction. Play and creativity are the language of children, and we believe when we enter that world with them, it can be an amazing place to cultivate skills and encourage empathy.

Imagination is a child's ability to visualize new ideas and concepts that aren't present in their physical reality, often through mental imagery.

Depending on the age, interests, and inner world of your child, how they express their creative imagination can manifest in a variety of ways. Some young children prefer more action-orientated play, such as clashing foam swords, finding lost treasures, or dancing in an imaginary ballroom.

Dramatic play consists of what you would traditionally associate with imaginative pretend play, such as using costumes and props in elaborate roleplays, making an imaginary meal, or hosting a tea party for each of their much-adored snuggly friends. Make-believe games are naturally enjoyable to young children and supports their understanding of themselves and the world around them. Playing with a variety of toys can also help your child find new ways to express themselve, find connections with others and understand the world around them.

Around the age of three and older, children will begin to transition from independent imaginative play to engaging with their preschool peers. They may roleplay as parents or conjure up a storyline in which they must escape a monster by hopping on one foot.

This is also the time when children will learn how to play with others, which can involve:

- Respecting others' space
- Learning to identify and express their emotions
- Regulating their emotions when feeling hurt

Through their play and interaction with others, you have a wonderful backdrop to help them start to learn the skills they need as well as have a place to practice. A child's interest in social play may start to be higher at this time because the drive to connect with others and have good experiences becomes more important to them.

AFFIRMATION

I know deep inside,
I can create what I feel.
When I enter my dream world,
I can make anything real.

Importance of Imagination in Child Development

Imagination and creativity in the early years of childhood is paramount to your child's mental and emotional health. Many times we see this coming through in play. Through play and imagination, children can gain valuable skills.

When children engage in imaginative play, it can help them become aware that their thoughts and perspectives may differ from other children, which can be a way to start to grasp concepts of empathy. When they explore dramatic play, it can support them in developing cognitive flexibility—the ability to adapt the way they think, behave, and respond based on what's happening in the world around them. It also lets them try on new roles and understand their likes and dislikes. As children enter a world of fantasy, they are allowed to express a wide range of emotions and don't have to "own" them so directly. It allows them to see and witness differing thoughts, feelings, and emotions from a distance that allows more processing.

How to Encourage Imagination in Children

Creativity often comes naturally to children. However, many conditions in our lives—like systematic oppression, socioeconomic conditions, and experienced trauma—can discourage creative expression, particularly when children's fight-or-flight responses are activated.

To create a safe place in which your children can express themselves freely, your communication and availability can do wonders. We encourage parents to regularly engage with their children and enter their worlds. You could discuss what they are seeing—such as the color of the leaves—or carve out time for storytelling and join them in making up stories together. When you engage with them, you are showing them that you are a trusted person to share their inner world with.

Many times children will lead you in the creative play, all you need to do is strap in and follow their lead. But if your child is having some "stuckness" around creativity, you could support some of these ideas to inspire creativity:

- Spending time outdoors
- Reading bedtime stories
- Presenting paints, clays, and crayons
- Encouraging active play
- Introducing musical instruments
- Engaging in verbal activities like I Spy
- Asking open-ended questions
- Limiting screen time
- Scheduling unstructured time for exploration
- Engaging them with activity boxes

There are so many things that we, as caregivers, can offer children that support their imagination:

Unstructured downtime: These days, it seems like every minute of our lives is scheduled, and we know how tempting it can be to do the same for our children. We get it. . .we all want the best for our kiddos and to give them as many opportunities as possible. However, carving out unstructured time for play is essential for supporting not only their imagination but their independence and growth as well. The next time your child says they're bored, let them lead the charge in deciding what to do. By encouraging them to embrace boredom, they learn to entertain themselves, developing interests that may even turn into passions as they grow.

Joining your kids in the play: What better way to encourage play and imagination than by setting an example yourself? Jump into role-playing with your child or let them take the lead in creating a made-up game. Playing with another person teaches children important social skills like collaboration and compromises. When you play together, children can practice identifying and responding to your feelings. This is a great opportunity to learn skills like empathy and conflict resolution!

Open-ended toys: Open-ended toys offer space for children to explore and create using their imagination. With the freedom to play without any structure or expectations, children are inspired to make up stories and create their own rules. Here's more good news: there are countless open-ended toys out there. Examples include art supplies, cars, dolls, creatures (like your favorite Slumberkin!), and objects found in nature. Open-ended toys can also help children process and express their emotions. They might use them to work through an event or a new situation. You might be surprised by how long these objects will keep your child engaged, but here's the truth: there's nowhere a child's imagination can't take them.

Imagination is a beautiful thing. It lets us share stories, shapes our relationship to others and to ourselves, and helps us make sense of the world around us. By encouraging your child's imagination, you're giving them the chance to learn and practice key skills that'll support them throughout their lives.

AFFIRMATION

I feel bored. That's okay.
There is so much I can do.
I can use how I feel
to create something new.

PARENT REFLECTION MOMENT: CREATIVITY

Creativity may not be a topic that stops you in your tracks due to a conflict, but it sure can be a life-giving force to reflect on. Here are some ways to tune into your own creativity and beliefs around creativity to help you show up with more openness to your own endeavors and those of your child.

Here are some questions to consider if you would like to implement our CALM Moment with a focus on Creativity. You can return to Chapter 5, pages 98–100 ("CALM Moments") to have an outline of this process as you engage in the following Reflection Questions.

In moments of struggle, when seeking clarity and self-comfort, ponder these questions:

- How can I empathize with my child's feelings while encouraging them to explore creative solutions?
- What support did I receive when I felt bored as a child, and how can I offer similar support to my child now?

For broader reflection on creativity and boredom:

- What activities am I excited to engage in with my child?
- How did I experience boredom as a child, and how does it manifest for me as an adult?
- How can I support my child in navigating their emotions, including boredom?

Things to Remember

- Creativity is the courage to explore, to ask questions, and to express yourself in unique ways.
- Creativity can be a nurturing and effective tool to support a child with challenges.
- Unstructured free time (which may lead to boredom) is essential.
- Through imaginative play, children can learn about the world around them and cultivate their creative thinking skills.

SLUMBERKINS CHARACTER CONNECTION: DRAGON

USE CASE GUIDE

This guide is meant to be a shortcut to the areas of information that will support the stage or situation you are in. As an educator and therapist, we are often asked by parents and community members what we'd recommend based on their family's unique needs or situations. We approached making this chart the same way we would when giving those personal recommendations. Though this guide is fairly comprehensive, every family is unique and parenting is very complex, and there may be some situations that we did not capture.

You might not see some topics that are very common in other parenting books (i.e., potty training, sleep training, feeding, etc.). Although these topics are important and a part of everyday parenting, this book is meant to support the *emotional development* of your child (and you) through these situations.

To search for recommendations for a particular situation, first find the general age of the child or adult in question on the left, then refer to the chapters listed on the right. We've also included a list of situational recommendations for all ages at the bottom.

We hope this guide gives you multiple strategies to encourage positive change in your child's life, and your life, as well.

325

INFANT

New Baby	Routines, Mindfulness, Gratitude
Adoption	Building Connections, Routines, Gratitude
New Sibling	Change, Gratitude, Building Connections
Secure Attachments	Routines, Building Connections

TODDLER + PRESCHOOL AGE

Increased Independence	Routines, Self-Esteem, Self-Acceptance, Self-Expression
Bedtime Routine Support	Routines, Anxiety
Affirming Self + Identity	Authenticity, Self-Acceptance, Self-Esteem, Emotional Courage
Sibling Rivalry	Conflict Resolution, Growth Mindset, Self-Expression (to support setting boundaries with each other)
Tantrums/Frustration/ Anger/Biting/Hitting	Conflict Resolution, Self-Expression, Self-Acceptance, Emotional Courage, Routines
Building Empathy	Self-Esteem, Emotional Courage, Mindfulness, Gratitude
Deeply Feeling/Highly Sensitive Kids	Emotional Courage, Mindfulness, Self-Expression, Anxiety
Physically Busy or Dysregulated Kids	Mindfulness, Emotional Courage, Routines, Creativity
Calming Skills	Mindfulness, Emotional Courage, Conflict Resolution
Starting Preschool	Growth Mindset, Routines, Change
Building Social Skills	Growth Mindset, Self-Esteem, Authenticity, Self-Acceptance, Conflict Resolution
Shyness	Self-Esteem, Creativity, Self-Expression
Play + Imagination	Creativity, Mindfulness
Problem-Solving + Flexible Thinking Skills	Growth Mindset, Self-Acceptance, Creativity, Conflict Resolution
Perfectionism/Welcoming (Making) Mistakes	Self-Acceptance, Self-Esteem, Growth Mindset
Consent/Personal Safety Boundaries	Self-Expression, Emotional Courage
Separation Anxiety	Anxiety, Change, Routines, Building Connections

BIG KID + ELEMENTARY SCHOOL AGE

Starting School	Routines, Building Connections, Growth Mindset
Setting Boundaries	Self-Expression, Emotional Courage
Emotional Safety	Authenticity, Emotional Courage, Self-Expression
Peer Conflict	Conflict Resolution, Self-Esteem, Growth Mindset, Self-Expression
Peer Pressure/Fitting In	Authenticity, Emotional Courage
Shyness	Self-Esteem, Creativity, Authenticity
Coping with Hurt Feelings or Bullying	Self-Esteem, Self-Expression, Authenticity
Discussing Discrimination	Self-Esteem, Authenticity, Building Connections
Feeling Different/Unique	Self-Esteem, Authenticity
Anxious Child	Self-Esteem, Anxiety, Emotional Courage, Mindfulness, Creativity, Gratitude
Academic Difficulty	Growth Mindset, Self-Esteem, Self-Acceptance
Comparison to Others/ Insecurity	Authenticity, Self-Esteem, Emotional Courage
Doing the Hard/Right Thing	Emotional Courage, Self-Expression, Authenticity
Unconditional Love	Authenticity, Self-Acceptance, Self-Esteem, Building Connections, Gratitude
Goal Setting/Manifesting	Creativity, Growth Mindset, Routines

ADULT/PARENTING

Postpartum Anxiety or Depression	Anxiety, Self-Expression, Emotional Courage, Building Connections
Co-Parenting/Parenting Conflicts	Conflict Resolution, Self-Expression, Emotional Courage, Change, Building Connections
Parenting Guilt or Shame	Self-Acceptance, Self-Esteem, Growth Mindset, Emotional Courage
Gentle/Mindful Parenting	Mindfulness, Gratitude
Single/Solo Parenting	Building Connections, Anxiety, Self-Acceptance, Self-Expression, Creativity
Parent-Child Conflict	Conflict Resolution, Emotional Courage, Self-Expression
Embracing Cultures and Community	Building Connections, Authenticity
Family Values + Belief Systems	Building Connections, Authenticity, Emotional Courage
Relationships and Family Systems	Building Connections
Foster Parenting	Building Connections, Change, Grief and Loss
Military Families	Change, Building Connections
Judgment from other Parents or Family	Self-Acceptance, Growth Mindset, Authenticity, Self-Expression
Blended Families	Building Connections, Authenticity, Change, Conflict Resolution, Self-Expression
Same-Sex Parenting or LGBTQ Allyship	Authenticity, Building Connections, Self-Expression

SITUATIONAL

Moving + New School	Building Connections, Change, Grief and Loss
Separation/Divorce	Change, Building Connections, Grief and Loss
Death of a Loved One	Grief and Loss, Change, Building Connections, Emotional Courage, Creativity
Trauma Support	Change, Grief and Loss, Anxiety, Creativity
Abuse	Self-Expression, Anxiety, Emotional Courage Creativity
Chronic Illness	Change, Anxiety, Grief and Loss, Creativity
Extended Separation (COVID, Long-distance Family, Unexpected Health Issues)	Change, Anxiety, Building Connections
Loss of Ability	Change, Grief and Loss, Change, Self-Acceptance

INDEX

Page numbers followed by *f* refer to figures.

Attachment relationships
(*Continued*)
fearful-avoidant (disorganized),
17–18, 20–21
primary, 16–17
Attachment styles, 17, 19–21, 23,
30
Authenticity. *See also* Unicorn
character
building, 196–197
in clown personality type, 44
and connection to self, 65
and creativity, 314
exploring, 191–194
fostering, 194–195
and healthy bonding, 130
and mindfulness, 142
mirroring, 71
and self-expression, 300–301
and Unicorn character, 104

Baumeister, Roy, 125
Bedtime routines, 115–121
Belonging:
and authenticity, 194–195, 199
to community, 30
and connection building, 102,
125–128
promoting sense of,
129–130
and self-reflection, 73, 134
and social self-care, 29
struggling with, 132–133

Bigfoot character, 46, 104, 180,
188. *See also* Self-esteem
Bonds:
to chosen families, 126–127
and co-parenting, 256
with family, 130–131
in grief process, 280
healthy, 130–131
importance of, 15
repairing, 70
and secure attachments, 17, 21,
129–130
and separation anxiety, 270
and sleep routines, 116
Boundaries:
for abuse prevention, 306
and anxiety, 265–266
with babies, 28
of caregiver personality type, 46
emotional, 307–308
and emotional courage, 162
in grief process, 281–282, 291
importance of, 300–301
lack of, 248
with peers, 238
physical, 306–307
during potty training, 32–33
and self-care, 29
and self-expression, 106,
303–304, 309
setting, 297–299, 305–308
with siblings, 237
and social norms, 115

INDEX

Page numbers followed by *f* refer to figures.

in Stop, Think, Choose method, 305–306

during tantrums, 236

Break taking, 43, 210

Brown, Brene', 191

CALM approach to parenting, 98–101, 257–258

and anxiety, 274

and authenticity, 208

for change, 257

and conflict resolution, 240

and connection building, 134

and creativity, 322

and emotional courage, 162, 174

and gratitude, 174

and grief and loss, 293

and growth mindset, 213

and mindfulness, 148

and routines, 121

and self-acceptance, 225

and self-esteem, 187

and self-expression, 187

Caregiver (helper) personality type, 46

Caring Crew, 101f, 102–103

CDC-Kaiser Permanente adverse childhood experiences study, 126

Centering, 98, 257. See also CALM approach to parenting

Change, 245–259. See also Fox character

in behavior, 133

and CALM method, 257–258

in family systems, 247–249

with new siblings, 249–251

with separation and divorce, 257

supporting, 245–247

Child-centered play therapy, 9

Chosen families, 126

Clown personality type, 48–49

Community:

and belonging, 125, 129

building connections in, 135

childrens' connection to, 126–128

connection to Lynx character, 106

connection to Otter character, 102, 135

definition of, 30–31

participation in, 173

in schools, 168

support groups in, 292

Comparison, 184, 196, 222, 316

Confidence Crew, 103–105, 103f

Confidence posture, 186

Conflict resolution, 229–241. See also Hammerhead character

among peers, 237–239

components of, 229–231

and sibling rivalry, 237

for tantrums, 231–234

confident postures, 185
co-regulation, 232
creating secure relationships, 15
educational, 23
emotional courage, 195
gratitude, 103, 167–169,
    171–174
grieving, 280
mindfulness, 139–140,
    143–144, 148
mirroring, 72
and play, 321–322
reflection, 71, 99
self-acceptance, 219–223
self-compassion, 222
self-connection, 64
self-reflection, 74
setting boundaries, 298–299,
    309
taking breaks, 210
Predictability, 111–112, 114, 116,
    119, 245, 268. *See also*
    Consistency; Routines
Primary attachment relationships,
    16–17. *See also*
    Attachment relationships
Professional guidance, 161, 273
Prolonged grief disorder (PGD),
    280

Reassurance:
    for anxious children, 18, 268
    from community, 31
    during divorce, 253

during grief periods, 291–292
from routine, 115
in secure attachment, 17
for self-esteem issues, 185
and separation anxiety, 269–270
through physical touch, 27
Reflection, 71–77
    on anxiety, 274–275
    on attachment styles, 19
    and authenticity, 192, 195,
        199–200
    during CALM moments, 98–100
    on change, 257–259
    and conflict resolution, 234,
        240–241
    on connections, 134–135
    on core beliefs, 56–57
    on emotional courage, 162–163
    encouraging, 301
    on gratitude, 174–175
    on grief and loss, 293–294
    on growth mindset, 213–214
    in highly sensitive children, 159
    kids' perspective on, 72–74
    on mindfulness, 148
    and mirroring, 71–72
    and modeling, 74–77
    opportunities for, 6
    on routines, 121–122
    self-(*see* Self-reflection)
    and self-acceptance, 220,
        225–226
    on self-esteem, 187–188
    on self-expression, 308–309

Validation of emotions. *See also*
Positive reinforcement
about new siblings, 251
during divorce, 253
and emotional courage, 154
of highly sensitive
children, 160
by listening, 213, 268, 302
positive, 197
and self-esteem, 197
and self-exploration, 197
and separation anxiety, 270

using mindfulness, 140
using words of encouragement
in, 207

Withdrawal, from social situations, 132, 251, 303.
See also Shyness

Yak character, 45, 105, 226. *See
also* Self-acceptance
Yeti character, 102, 121. *See also*
Mindfulness